D0252954

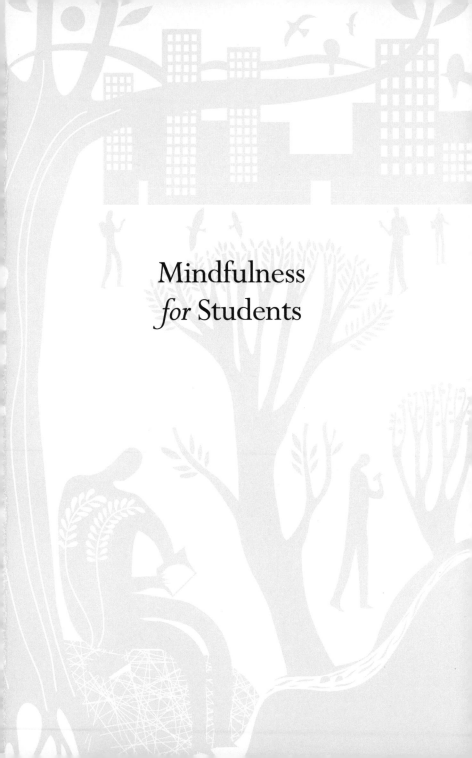

Mindfulness
for Students

Mindfulness
for Students

Embracing now, looking to the future

Natasha Kaufman

Leaping Hare Press

First published in the UK in 2019 by

Leaping Hare Press

An imprint of The Quarto Group
The Old Brewery, 6 Blundell Street
London N7 9BH, United Kingdom
T (0)20 7700 6700 **F** (0)20 7700 8066
www.QuartoKnows.com

Text © 2019 Natasha Kaufman
Design and layout © 2019 Quarto Publishing plc

British Library Cataloguing-in-Publication Data
A catalogue record for this book is available from the British Library

ISBN: 978-1-78240-767-6

This book was conceived, designed and produced by

Leaping Hare Press

58 West Street, Brighton BN1 2RA, United Kingdom
Publisher SUSAN KELLY
Editorial Director TOM KITCH
Art Director JAMES LAWRENCE
Project Editor STEPHANIE EVANS
Design Manager ANNA STEVENS
Designer GINNY ZEAL
Illustrator MELVYN EVANS

Printed in China

1 3 5 7 9 10 8 6 4 2

CONTENTS

INTRODUCTION

*Life can be tough. With key decisions to
make at a crucial time, from subject choices
to new colleges and universities, careers and
relationships, it's easy to feel weighed down. What's
more, there's the pressure to gain good grades, find
a good job and be a good person. From a young age, we
are taught the significance of a solid education and a
fruitful career, yet with such emphasis on academic
and monetary success we are failing to achieve a
healthy mind. Leaving the security of home and
adjusting to new-found independence can be an
exciting transition. It can also be unsettling. It is vital
to know how to deal with challenges and triumphs
emotionally. Practising mindfulness can
equip you with the skills to do this.*

WHY BE MINDFUL?

◆

Mindfulness is a mental state of being in the present moment. By practising mindful meditations or being mindful in your daily routine, you can gain a sense of perspective and learn to acknowledge thoughts and feelings with acceptance. You will be able to live life in the moment, enjoying positive experiences and coping much better with stressful ones.

IT IS IMPORTANT TO BECOME AWARE of what you are feeling mentally and physically without wanting to try to change your thoughts or feelings. Simply acknowledge the way things are in the present moment, knowing that everything changes and nothing stays the same. A thought passes, a feeling subsides; much like an inhalation and exhalation, it comes and goes. When we start applying this idea to everyday life, an issue that feels hard to tackle can be seen for what it is – a moment in time that will pass.

It might seem at times that there is no escape from our stresses and worries. These feelings can be exacerbated if we are constantly attached to our phones, which can lead to a detachment from our sense of selves. Whether we feel scrutinized by the expectations of our society, culture, peers or social media, we often judge and feel judged. When we learn to be mindful, we can become more self-accepting and we may find we become less judgemental of others.

For students, the fast pace of life, the pressure to succeed and get a job, and the anonymous and isolating aspects of communication through social media make mindfulness all the more relevant. You might recognize that it's easy to become introverted or go over the top (depending on your personality and social confidence), indulging in excessive drinking, eating badly or skipping sleep, and ignoring mental and physical signs of stress. Yet as much as this may seem like an overwhelming time it is also a valuable one. There are opportunities to connect with like-minded individuals and to become immersed in a subject you love. For many, the student experience is a rite of passage from their teens and family life to adulthood and independence. Whatever your experience as a student, there are mindful practices that you can learn that cost nothing but that can make your transition smooth and life-affirming.

Like our bodies, which need to be nourished with a balanced diet and regular exercise, we also need to replenish our minds. Just as a tightly toned physique isn't achieved overnight, neither is a mindful state. The first time we try to meditate it may feel frustrating, dull and pointless. Nevertheless, with patience and perseverance, what initially feels like a chore will eventually feel natural and effortless. When we consistently practise mindfulness, it can help reduce stress, anxiety and depression, and improve concentration, clarity and self-control.

This book aims to introduce you to the many benefits of mindfulness by looking at different ways to be mindful: breathing, eating, exercising, resting, studying and communicating. There will be opportunities within each chapter to have a go at mindful meditations that take between a mere three and up to 20 minutes. There is no right or wrong approach, just what works for you. This book can not only help you to pass your exams or do well in a job interview, but it will also teach you how to live your life now and in the future. Mindfulness is a way of being. You can choose to be mindful and to live your life being in the moment, living fully and wholeheartedly, aware of yourself and others.

WHERE DID MINDFULNESS ORIGINATE?

The buzz around mindfulness is spreading, through conversations, news reports, social feeds and adverts. It is making headlines in the West now, but Eastern cultures and religions have been practising mindfulness for thousands of years. Why has it taken Western communities so long to reap the rewards of this ancient philosophy?

MINDFULNESS BEGINS FROM A RELIGIOUS and spiritual place, although in the West it is predominantly practised from a non-religious angle. Its origins are in Hinduism and Buddhism. Elements of mindfulness have been interwoven with Hinduism for centuries. Age-old Hindu scriptures focus on acceptance, silence and meditation, which are at the core of mindfulness. The aim of meditation is to lose the ego and to allow the mind to reach a state of calmness so it can fully experience the beauty and wholeness of God. Today, people who do not follow any religion also meditate. They are not trying to experience the wholeness of God but of themselves. Jon Kabat-Zinn, a leading pioneer in mindfulness

McDonaldization

Populations around the globe are now at the crux of 'McDonaldization', a term coined by sociologist George Ritzer. Industrialized societies have become as fast paced as a fast-food chain, with the need for results in as little time as possible. We want our burger or chicken nuggets with extra fries and we want them now. Although we feel satisfied when we take our first bite, in a few hours we are hungry again. We think that the bigger our burger is, the better we will feel. But can quantity replace quality? Just like our lives, which move at the same rapid speed as the service at fast-food restaurants, we are losing the ability to wait a bit and to savour our meal. As a result, we may end up leaving full but still unsatisfied. It's important that we regroup, think again and re-evaluate how we have decided to live our lives.

meditation, brought the practice into mainstream medicine in 1979. He argues that we are often unaware of our own sense of worth. Perhaps this lack of completeness and self-fulfilment is because we are rarely taught the importance of tuning into ourselves and realizing we are just right, just as we are.

Although there are elements of mindfulness embodied in Hinduism, this form of meditation has truly grown and flourished within Buddhism. It is believed in Buddhism that the first stages of Enlightenment can be reached by practising mindfulness, and mindfulness meditation is very much engrained in Buddhist customs. The word 'mindfulness' comes from the word *sati* in the old Pali language of India. *Sati,* an important part of Buddhist traditions, captures the idea of awareness, attention and remembering. However, 'remembering' is not used as we may understand it, for example, to remember past events, but to remember to be aware and pay attention every moment.

We can draw comfort from the fact that this form of meditation has successfully been practised for thousands of years. Nevertheless, there is a problem with believing that Eastern religions have the answers, as if they had magical powers. We don't have to consider mindful meditation as something that is exotic, 'other' or even exciting but rather as a way of being that can work for all of us. The notion that this wisdom is in us and that we can benefit from it has been scientifically proven.

THE RESEARCH BEHIND THE REALITY

◆

Valid scientific experiments prove that our brains have the ability to change and grow. This gives us a huge incentive to improve and develop how we think and behave.

I MAGINE IF SOMEONE TOLD YOU that you could change the way you react, think, concentrate, form relationships and make decisions. You could increase your capacity to bear and accept pain or discomfort, and rise above the worries, stresses, anxieties and sufferings of life. Scientific research in the last 10 to 15 years has proven that this is possible. It has been found that the brain is an organ that can change and is constantly restructuring based on experiences. The scientific term for this is neuroplasticity. The findings are that the brain can be remoulded and reshaped.

As part of an experiment, the brains of meditators and non-meditators were scanned. The results of the Magnetic Resonance Imaging (MRI) showed that those who had taken part in an eight-week mindfulness course had improved their brains' functionality. The part of the brain that responds to fear and emotion, the amygdala, appeared to have shrunk. This part of the brain is associated with our innate response to stress and if it shrinks, this suggests we can actually improve how we instinctively respond to stressful situations. What's more, as the amygdala shrinks, the prefrontal cortex, the part of the brain that is associated with higher-order functions such as decision-making, concentration and awareness, actually becomes thicker. A thicker prefrontal cortex means our brain can make clearer decisions, concentrate for longer periods and be more aware. The extent of these changes depends on how regularly people meditate.

Ultimately, the results prove that meditation decreases stress levels and strengthens clarity, creativity and concentration. We don't need to turn to drugs or medical intervention to improve our abilities or limits. With effort and patience, we can restructure how our brain works. Think about what you could achieve if you were able to focus that bit longer or quickly overcome emotions that would once consume you. Science has proven that it is possible. You can improve and change how you work, think, react, focus and live your life. Only you know if you are willing to make the effort to do so.

Why Do We Act the Way We Do?

◆

Sometimes what is happening in our subconscious spurs us to behave in a certain manner. If we know ourselves, we can understand better how our minds operate.

WHEN I WAS YOUNGER, if I was ever slightly moody, angry or sullen, it would drive me mad when an adult said, 'That's such typical adolescent behaviour'. It was as if all young adults were boxed into the same category just because of our changing hormones. I know for sure I never felt like a teenager. I thought I was 19 going on 45. I was mature, worldly and hung out with friends twice my age. I felt that accusations of teenage behaviour really didn't apply to me.

As much as I was in denial that I ever went through a typical teenage phase, I couldn't escape the fact that my mind and brain had their own thing going. Even though I had friends, I remember always questioning whether they actually wanted me around. I had this constant voice in my head saying, 'Nobody likes you'. I was also hopelessly indecisive. When I arrived at university, I changed my course five times

Dopamine can seductively invite you to live life on the edge of danger

before I committed to my degree. I had insecurities that I became obsessed with. And yet, when I went travelling during my gap year, I was daringly spontaneous and adventurous, always brushing against danger with a sense of triumph and exhilaration.

I didn't know it at the time, but my impulsive behaviour was triggered by the release of the hormone dopamine. Dopamine can seductively invite you to live on the edge of danger because when it is produced, the rational evaluation of risk factors is thrown right out of the window, which is exactly what I experienced during one memorable summer trip.

A Brush with Danger

When I was at university, I went to Central America with some friends. We spent a day sunbathing on a beach and as our faces turned a crispy red, the sun started to go down. We were miles from our accommodation, and with no taxi in sight, we thought the obvious thing to do was to hitch-hike. We stood on the corner of a dirt road for about half an hour then a truck pulled up – one that had an open cart attached to the back. In the cart were five bare-chested men festooned with tattoos. With a subtle, approving nod to each other we climbed into the cart. In our heads we could hear the faint cry of our mothers screaming, 'What do you think you're doing? You fools!' Of course, that voice was quickly silenced.

I had travelled widely and believed I had a sixth sense. I thought I could smell danger and in my head, this ride was not dangerous – it was quite thrilling. As we sat on the floor of the cart, wind blowing in our hair and bodies jolting up and down as we drove over rocky roads, the men were eyeing us up. Admittedly, we did feel a bit uncomfortable. We had been warned about the serious dangers of hitch-hiking, especially as young female tourists, but we were more concerned with getting a free ride. Luckily, we arrived safely back at our accommodation, but this story could have gone in many ways.

What possessed us to risk our lives? Would I take such a risk as I did in Central America today? No way! That's partly because those hedonistic, wild days are long gone. But more importantly, I would truly question and weigh up the risks and very quickly, that spontaneous urge would be knocked into sense.

I hope none of you reading this are as foolish as I was, but you may relate to the desire to push aside what you know is right or wrong. You also may have a wild streak waiting to be unleashed or perhaps it is in full throttle. You too may have an inner critic who is always telling you aren't good enough. That's because although we may believe that we are ready for the big, wide world we still have some developing to do.

WHAT'S REALLY GOING ON INSIDE YOUR HEAD?

Everyone develops differently and at different times. The growth of the brain depends on many factors: gender, biological or genetic conditions as well as cultural, environmental and social experiences. Yet the framework and functions may work in similar ways for healthy young adults.

YOU DON'T NEED TO KNOW exactly how each part of the brain performs, but having some insight into just a few key components may shed some light on your behaviours, thoughts and actions.

Prefrontal Cortex

Your prefrontal cortex is the part of the brain that is linked with reasoning, decision making, planning and social behaviour. It doesn't fully develop until you reach your mid-twenties and sometimes, before it has entirely formed, decision making may seem hard. Instead you may rely more on the limbic system, the part of your brain that is responsible for emotions, memories and arousal. *As a result, you may not always think before you speak or act* because your reactions are based on feelings rather than reason. However, this impulsiveness changes once the prefrontal cortex is fully linked with other parts of the brain. This increases your ability to empathize, choose, resolve, plan effectively and form strategies.

The Amygdala

The amygdala (which is within the limbic system) is the part of the brain responsible for memory, impulses, survival instincts and emotions. Like the prefrontal cortex it doesn't fully develop until your mid-twenties. You may find it hard to process emotions since this is the part of the brain that helps to regulate and control feelings. Instead of using the prefrontal cortex to rationalize your responses, you may find that you respond to situations from an instinctual or 'gut' feeling because the amygdala overrides the rational part of the brain. Just as the amygdala can lead to you acting spontaneously or taking risks, it also encourages you to seek new experiences, and to be independent and creative.

Hormones

During puberty, you may have found that everyone was constantly mentioning the word 'hormones' or talking about being 'hormonal'. You may have used it as a legitimate excuse for your mood swings, actions or emotions. Even when puberty has officially passed, these chemicals in your body still like to work their magic and can have a dramatic effect on how you feel, think and act. Here are the main ones.

Cortisol

Cortisol controls a variety of processes throughout the body, including the regulation of the immune system and metabolism. It is also responsible for how the body responds to stress since it is released during moments of pressure, anxiety or fear. If you frequently feel stressed, large amounts of cortisol will be released in the body, which can have negative effects on how you sleep, eat and function day to day. Too much cortisol can be disruptive to your mental and physical health. You can naturally lower cortisol levels by sleeping more, eating regular meals rather than snacking, walking and exposing yourself to sunlight daily.

Serotonin

Serotonin is a chemical messenger (known as a neurotrans-mitter) that sends information throughout your brain and body. It helps maintain mood stability, sleeping patterns and digestion. It is also known as the 'happy hormone' and flows through our bodies when we feel loved, important and valued. If we are lacking in this vital hormone, it can lead to feelings of aggression, edginess and restlessness, and low mood. Sleep patterns can also be affected if serotonin levels aren't right, and you may crave more sugars and carbs. Fortunately, lifestyle changes such as exercising, meditating and eating a good diet can boost serotonin levels and help you feel at ease and content.

Dopamine

Dopamine is also a neurotransmitter that sends signals to nerve cells in the body. This chemical can influence your emo-tions, motor skills and your feelings of pleasure and pain. There are many dopamine pathways in the brain, and one of these contributes to reward-motivated behaviour. If we antici-pate a reward owing to our actions, dopamine levels in the brain are increased, and this can make us feel particularly good about ourselves. The release of dopamine is a pleasur-able feeling that can give us a buzz. Due to the feel-good factor of dopamine, it can tempt you to be courageous, adven-turous and a risk taker. However, dopamine deficiency can occur if we consume too much caffeine, alcohol, or sugar. Stress can also deplete dopamine. Low dopamine levels can cause fatigue, lack of motivation, inability to experience joy, forgetfulness, insomnia and mood swings. There are ways that dopamine levels can rebalance themselves. These include exercise, exposure to more sunlight (for vitamin D) and taking certain vitamins such as B5 and B6.

Adrenalin

The main job of the hormones adrenalin and noradrenalin is to prepare us for 'fight or flight' (see chapter two). In times of stress, this can cause us to act quickly or with intense vigour. Faced with highly competitive or threatening situations, your

---

Benefits of Mindfulness

- Improves self-control
- Enhances creativity, clarity and concentration
- Gives you a deeper appreciation for life
- Decreases anxiety, stress and depression
- Increases empathy and compassion
- Improves relationships
- Lessons frets about the future
- Diminishes past regrets
- Strengthens, trains and develops the brain.

adrenalin really kicks in. You will know when adrenalin is released because your heart rate and breathing will speed up. This feeling can make you feel energized, excited and alert. During exam season it is usually adrenalin that keeps you going and gives you the extra drive and ability to work longer hours.

When you regularly practise mindfulness meditation, you can develop and grow the brain to benefit your mental well-being. Surely, as your brain is still developing, now is the best time to adopt this skill. This book isn't about sitting still in a lotus position waiting for a Zen-like transformation but it does suggest realistic ways you can achieve a mindful outlook.

How to Use This Book

Hopefully, this introduction has helped you to understand why being mindful is so important. But reading and reading about mindfulness won't change much; it is something that you have to try for yourself.

I RECOMMEND STARTING WITH THE FIRST CHAPTER on how to breathe to help you build a foundation for meditating and being mindful. The following chapters don't have to be read in order – you can dip in and out of the practices as and when it suits you. You may find that there are certain ideas that you want to revisit at different moments in your life. Whatever you are practising, try to be open-minded and allow your experiences to unfold without judgement.

Summaries of Chapters

Breathe: A focus on using the breath to reduce feelings of stress and anxiety. How this can help with exams, concentration and clearing the mind.

Thought for Food: What you eat is of great importance; however, how you eat is equally as important. Learning to eat with intention and attention.

Switching Off: An emphasis on switching off phones, quietening thoughts and encouraging a better sleep and waking routine. Relaying how vital it is to 'switch off', especially when you are weighed down by exams and other pressures.

Tuning In: Paying attention to sounds and thoughts to start to calm and focus the mind. How being aware of the world around you and within can prevent negative thoughts. How mindful listening can improve focus and empathy.

Know Yourself: Meditations that focus on body awareness and mindful exercises. The significance of connecting with yourself and being in the moment, even when doing everyday tasks such as walking.

Compassion: Compassion fosters emotional intelligence and well-being. Focus on relationships, kindness and understanding of yourself and others.

Stress-Less: How to deal with stresses and anxieties by using a variety of different mindful meditations, which have been suggested throughout the book. Finding the most useful way to regularly apply these meditations.

CHAPTER ONE

BREATHE

*To be able to use something that happens
naturally as a way to navigate and cope with
moments of stress or anxiety is invaluable. Learning
to use the breath to anchor you back to the present
moment when you need it most can help you gain
perspective and a sense of calm. It sounds so easy and
so basic. Simply focus on your breath and your worries
may begin to evaporate. Surprisingly, this single
act can be difficult to practise at first but
once mastered you've gained a skill for life.*

OVERCOMING PERSONAL OBSTACLES

◆

To learn to meditate or to be aware of each moment as it unfolds, one must start by paying attention to the breath. This is the basis for all forms of meditation. The breath's grounding effect has a transformative quality that can bring stillness and tranquillity even in the most distressing situations.

WHEN SITTING ON A CHAIR with the aim of focusing on your breath, you may suddenly become preoccupied with the tension in your shoulders, the hardness of the chair beneath you, an itch on your nose or the heat in the room. Your mind may have shifted to how uncomfortable you feel. These sensations may override your ability to stay focused on your breath. Likewise, you may start to think how useless you are at meditating, that this isn't for you, that it is pointless and won't change anything. Perhaps your mind is overflowing with random thoughts. It is as if you are subconsciously stopping yourself from progressing with the practice. And once this spiral of thoughts begins, it is extremely difficult to rein it in.

But the point of mindfulness is not to reach a special state. If you can bring awareness to the fact that you are thinking about thinking, then you are being mindful. Equally, the intention isn't necessarily to feel better but to be able to learn to sit with undesirable emotions, feelings and sensations.

In life, there will always be suffering. It is how you deal with it that sets you apart and helps you to survive. If you are trying to avoid or run away from unpleasant emotions, your feelings will simply be repressed and they will come out at other times, in other ways. To be able to bear, accept,

---

MINDFUL EXERCISE

FOCUSING ON YOUR BREATHING
SEVEN MINUTES

- Close your eyes.
- Inhale deeply. Notice how your inhalation starts with the rise of your belly and then moves up your chest, back and throat.
- Exhale. Notice how your exhalation moves down your body, past your throat, chest and stomach.
- Inhale through your nose and exhale through your mouth. Do this three times.
- Now breathe naturally, not trying to change or control your breath. Notice how you breathe without judgement.
- Pay attention to how your breath moves up and down your body for five minutes.
- Move this awareness to the whole body. Picture the whole body breathing. You are breathing as one unit. Hold this in mind for two minutes.

---

acknowledge and confront your pain is what you are taught when you meditate. Learning to accept and acknowledge unwelcome thoughts and emotions with kindness and non-judgement is a valuable skill that can be applied during life's unfavourable situations and experiences.

To help you sit with uncomfortable sensations, you could try to notice your thoughts and accept what you are feeling without the need to try and change it. Acknowledge that each moment brings a new experience.

You could use visualizations to help you focus on the breath. For example, imagine that your breath is like a balloon; as you inhale, it inflates and as you exhale it deflates. Alternatively, imagine two cups of water seamlessly pouring from one to the other. As you inhale and exhale the water passes from one cup to the other.

To Be or Not To Be

When your mind is buzzing and you are constantly bombarded with thoughts, pausing and focusing inwards rather than outwards can sometimes give you some clarity.

HUMANS ARE THE MOST ADVANCED species and our ability to think and solve problems sets us apart. As a student you are constantly reasoning, theorizing, analysing, evaluating, philosophizing, critiquing, reading and writing.

Learning is at the heart of everything you do, even if not always in the academic sense. You could be in a new relationship, discovering the ups and downs of communicating and being intimate, learning to drive or exploring a new area to live. The thirst for knowledge and your active analytical mind make life exciting.

It seems the more advanced we become, the more we are bombarded with choice and temptation. Our magnificent minds are in a continuous state of wander, rumination, worry and fantasy. This constant mind wandering is what neuroscientists have called the 'default mode'; it is what we do habitually and without thought. If you have a particularly busy mind, don't overanalyse or judge yourself for this. This is just what we humans do; we think and then we think some more.

Besides, our society fuels this constant mind activity. Education is based on questioning, answering and problem solving. Even outside the lecture hall, the searching never ceases: 'Which subject are you going to study?' or 'What do

---

When It All Feels Too Much

- Inhale through your nose so deeply that you can't breathe in any more.
- Exhale fully through your mouth.

---

you want to be when you're older?' or 'Are you going to choose a subject you enjoy or one that guarantees work and good pay?' If it's not bad enough that your own thoughts are jumping from one to another, your peers, parents and any other breathing being are also bombarding you with questions. You are never really given the chance to stop and slow down. Most of the time, you are in a continual goal-driven state of mind – the 'doing mode'. However, when you over-think you

You are never really given the chance to stop and slow down

may be left feeling deflated, dejected and disillusioned. When the 'doing mode' is in overdrive, it can lead to difficulties.

Going into overdrive

Sometimes when life doesn't turn out as we hope, we can feel emotionally punctured and desperately want to reverse our misfortunes. These feelings can occur from everyday situations, such as an argument or not being invited to a party,

---

Benefits of the 'doing mode'

- Pushes you to get things done
- Helps you solve tricky maths problems
- Encourages you to make plans
- Helps you to find answers to life issues.

> ### Disadvantages of the 'doing mode'
>
> • Feelings of inadequacy
>
> • Comparing yourself with others and feeling that you are not good enough
>
> • Judging yourself, by saying 'I'm so stupid' or 'I'm unattractive'
>
> • Dissatisfaction – for instance, always focusing on things you don't have.

to events that can have a bigger impact on our futures, for example, failing an exam or being rejected by someone. In such cases your 'doing mode' can be triggered into overdrive. You begin to question and analyse things that are wrong with you. You feel inadequate and filled with self-doubt because of the gulf between what you want and the reality. Used to analysing and evaluating, your mind begins to apply these skills to your life situation. You ask yourself: 'What have I done wrong?' 'If I lost a few kilos would she come back to me?' 'I always fail at tests – why does everyone else do better than me?'

Despite the fact that these situations may be out of your control, your mind frantically tries to think its way to a resolution. You become so fixated on what has gone wrong in the past and what could go wrong in the future that you lose all sense of what is going on in the present.

Furthermore, when you are feeling unhappy, stressed, anxious, fearful, disappointed or angry, your mind is searching for solutions and your thoughts are going round and round with no end in sight. You may begin to question why you aren't feeling happy and try to work out what you can do to feel better. But, by attempting to bridge the gap between what you want to feel and what you actually feel, you often end up feeling worse than you did in the first place. When these thoughts begin circulating, you may not be aware of this habitual way of thinking. In moments like these, there is an alternative state we can aim for, and this is the 'being mode'.

By attempting to bridge the gap between what you want to feel and what you actually feel, you often end up feeling worse than you did in the first place

To reap the benefits of the being mode and to experience what it feels like just to be, have a go at the brief exercise on the following page and focus on your breath for just three minutes.

Deciding To Be

If counting your breaths for three minutes seemed like an excruciating amount of time to focus on something that seems mundane, you are not alone. Most people find it hard when they first try meditating and going inwards rather than

COUNTING YOUR BREATH
THREE MINUTES

- Set a timer on your phone for three minutes and find a quiet place to sit.
- Bring awareness to the soles of your feet resting on the floor. Let the ground take your weight.
- Close your eyes and just notice the sensation of your breath.
- Take a slow and steady inhale and count 1 in your head.
- Notice the slight pause at the top of your breath.
- Exhale – count 2. Again, notice the brief pause.
- Steady inhale, count 3, pause.
- Exhale, count 4, pause.
- Inhale, count 5.
- When you reach 5, start again at 1.
- Keep repeating the steady and slow rhythmic counting of your breath until the timer stops.
- If thoughts flood your mind or you lose count, don't worry. It is natural to think. You are not trying to stop your thoughts. Just acknowledge what you are thinking or the fact your mind is racing. Let the thoughts pass without getting attached and without judgement. If you lose focus on your counting, go back to 1 and start again.

planning external goals. On the other hand, maybe you felt that was easy and calming. Whatever you felt during the three-minute exercise, don't label or judge yourself, either thinking 'I can't do this' or even 'I'm so good at this.' There is no right or wrong way of feeling.

Just by taking a few moments to make the conscious effort to step away from your current activity or ruminating thoughts, you are mindfully tapping into what is happening in the present moment. Hopefully, you will notice that your thoughts are not you; they are not occurring as you think them; they are not reality. All that is happening in this moment is the ebb and flow of your breath. Everything else can temporarily melt away. When you make the decision to be rather than to do, you can bring attention to the fact that you might be comparing, judging, planning or criticizing. If you notice your thought patterns, perhaps you can take comfort in the idea that as easily as they appear, they can also fade.

You can use your breath to ground you back to the experience of watching each moment unravel in real time

The 'doing mode' sends you forward to the future and back to the past. This can be useful. Being able to reflect on your previous actions and life experiences helps you to mature, while setting goals for the future gives you ambition

---

Benefits of the 'Being Mode'

- Gives you perspective
- Brings you back to an awareness of the present
- Allows things to be just as they are without you wanting to change anything
- Creates acceptance
- Gives you a sense of stillness and calm
- Reduces judgement
- Quietens your inner critic
- Stops you comparing yourself to others
- Allows you to appreciate what you do have rather than what you don't.

---

and motivation. But if you become entangled in what you haven't achieved and confused about what do in the future, you may need to process what is unfolding in the present to give you a sense of stability and acceptance of your feelings. During the time in which you pay attention to the present moment rather than worrying about the future or past, you may reach a feeling of freedom or relief. With an awareness of how your mind is in overdrive you can use your breath to ground you back to the experience of watching each moment unravel in real time.

How My Doing Mode
Drove Me to Indecisiveness

When I left university with a degree that didn't lead to a specific job, I faced the conundrum of what I was going to do with my life. It seemed that all my friends had it sorted. They had internships, training contracts or interesting jobs. They had a clear direction and they were sprinting towards their goals. I, on the other hand, was lagging far behind.

As a student, I was good at the Humanities. However, when you are just plain 'good', not exceptional or outstanding, it causes a dilemma. Not having a particular talent or skill meant I had choice, and with choice came confusion. I began searching the internet to find the perfect career and before I knew it, I had one hundred tabs and had entered into a bottomless pit of opportunities. Seeing all the paths I could take and not knowing which one would be the 'right decision' sent my mind into a frenzy. What was I going to do? Who was I going to be? My thoughts kept circulating and they stopped me from moving forward with clarity.

At one point, I was a teaching assistant in a primary school while doing a law convergence course and at the same time writing articles for a local newspaper. I was trying every avenue in the hope that it would lead me to where I wanted to be. Instead, by overthinking and overanalysing, I made myself anxious and puzzled. I couldn't step out of my head and I was so desperately trying to think my way to my future that I lost all sense of what was going on the present moment. My anxiety worsened as my indecisiveness deepened.

During times of inner crisis, I wish I had been able to tap into the stillness that I now know I can reach. Had I been able to realize that my thoughts had started to control my emotions and that they were damaging my confidence, I might have approached my career planning with the clarity that can be achieved in the being mode. When the doing mode is overstimulated with life decisions, you can choose to move away from this state and instead start to notice your thoughts, emotions and feelings as they arise. If I had been able to recognize that my thinking was becoming counterproductive, that by hypothesizing every possible scenario I was stopping myself from moving forward, I could have saved myself from turmoil.

> *By overthinking and overanalysing, I made myself anxious and puzzled ... My anxiety worsened as my indecisiveness deepened*

Life decisions never stop. There will always be different routes you can choose to take. Nowadays when confronted with a variety of options, I take a moment to tap into what I am feeling. By closing my eyes and focusing on the sensation of breathing for a few minutes, I try to anchor myself in the present moment, which helps me to break away from my circulating thoughts. Taking a break from worrying about the future or regretting actions in the past calms my nervous system. With a calmer outlook, I can usually gain the perspective I need to make a decision confidently.

REDUCING STRESS & ANXIETY

◆

Stress and anxiety are mentally and physically overwhelming emotions. At their worst, they can be debilitating. Learning to manage and recognize powerful feelings allows you to cope with adverse sensations.

STRESS CAN HIT YOU AT ANY TIME of the day: when you realize a deadline is looming; when you have to read a dozen articles just to understand one theory; when you lose your wallet; when you're late – the list is endless. When stress punches you with an angry 'hello', it raises your blood pressure, increases your heart rate and heats your face like a throbbing red bruise. Stress pops up and stands its ground with defiant arrogance. Yet once the stressful situation is over, often your heightened emotion diminishes. Anxiety, however, is not as amenable. Anxiety thuds repetitively at your heart, brings your nails to your mouth and makes you chomp them, rather like a squirrel devouring a nut. What's more, anxiety lingers and doesn't get the hint to leave, no matter how frequently you ask.

It is completely normal to feel stressed and anxious. These feelings are part of the human condition and, if channelled correctly, can give you drive and push you towards your goals. However, these emotions are exacerbated when we start feeding them stories – when we listen and become consumed with the limitless negative possibilities.

If you can become aware of your thoughts and the bodily sensations that stress and anxiety provoke, you can begin to let these overwhelming feelings pass on by. Yes, you have exams and they are stressful. You have life decisions to make. There is no denying that you are under a lot of pressure. But instead of focusing on the things you haven't done or need to do, pause and bring

> *It is completely normal to feel stressed and anxious. These feelings are part of the human condition*

awareness to your breath, posture and the sounds around you. You will soon realize that the persistent narrative of stressful thoughts is orchestrated by you. When you recognize that you are constructing the fabric of your thoughts, you can understand that the direction of these thoughts is up to you. Will they keep manifesting themselves or can you move them towards a more peaceful resolution?

Three-breath Relaxation

This technique can be applied at any moment and takes just seconds. It is a particularly effective method because it activates the parasympathetic nervous system, which can help to calm you down. It can bring you back to the present moment even in the most distressing situations.

When to use it

- Before an exam
- Before a driving test
- While writing an academic paper
- During a difficult conversation
- Before an interview
- While waiting for a bus or when you are late
- When going on a first date.

What to do

- Take a slow, deep breath in and out.
- Focus on how your exhalation leaves your body.
- Take a moment to feel grounded in the present moment.
- Picture your out breath reaching the floor and imagine that it evaporates beneath you.
- As it leaves your body, visualize that your stress exits too.
- Repeat three times.

Unfortunately, focusing on the sensation of breathing will not take away your deadlines but it does help you appreciate that you are doing all you can in the here and now. By stepping away from the verbal diarrhoea in your head, you can see that the circumstances in your life that cause you suffering are moments in time that will eventually change. If these situations move on by, why should you be frozen in deadlock?

Using a Breathing Mantra

A mantra is typically a repeated word or simple sound to help your concentrate during meditation. It can also be used to help reframe negative thinking. For example, 'I can pass my exams' or 'Everything is going to be OK' or 'Breath in, stress out'. You can choose any phrase or word that helps your mindset. Try to apply your chosen mantra to the rhythm of your breath. For example, inhale and say to yourself 'anxiety in' and exhale, saying 'anxiety out'. This can help steady your thoughts because concentrating on your breath gives you a clear focus.

By acknowledging your emotional state . . . you start a process of accepting how you feel rather than battling to defeat it

Additionally, by acknowledging your emotional state – stressed, anxious, sad or fearful – you start a process of accepting how you feel rather than battling to defeat it.

FIGHT, FLIGHT OR FREEZE

◆

Learning to recognize how we instinctively respond in fearful moments can help determine our automatic reactions. If we can use the breath to regain perspective and reduce feelings of panic, the apparent threat may become manageable.

HUMANS HAVE A NATURAL SURVIVAL MODE that is activated by our instinctive response to danger. When we sense an immediate threat, an automatic switch is turned on before we have a chance to think about the consequences. This response is caused by the activation of the amygdala, which triggers our fight, flight or freeze response.

In hunter-gatherer times, this was particularly relevant. Confronted with a tiger, you would naturally respond in order to survive: freeze and hope you wouldn't be seen; take flight and hide; fight – grab a spear to defend yourself. This quick assessment of danger could have saved your life. Nowadays, our threats may not be matters of life or death, yet our bodily response is the same. For many students, the thought of exams, public speaking, interviews or certain social situations can cause feelings of terror. How you naturally respond to these imposed threats may not be beneficial.

The thought of exams, public speaking, interviews or certain social situations can cause feelings of terror

A negative response to forthcoming exams could be:

Fight – overwork and burn yourself out

Flight – run away from your fears by partying, going on holiday or travelling

Freeze – avoid doing anything owing to a fear of failure.

Although the activation of the amygdala is necessary to survive in times of real danger, when it is overstimulated, circumstances that are bearable can become unbearable. It can result in a person becoming hypervigilant. They scan the world for potential threats, and even everyday situations can cause a sense of panic. This overzealous worry can lead to panic attacks.

If this happens, mindfulness can help you be less reactive and to recognize when you have entered into a high-alert zone. You can follow the simple breathing exercise above to shift out of an overcautious state.

Using the Breath to Cope with Panic

- Breathe in through the nose for a count of two breaths.
- Exhale fully through the mouth for a count of four breaths.
- Repeat until you feel a sense of calmness.
- Locate where you can feel sensations of panic. Is it in your heart or the back of your throat? Is there tightness in your chest? Breathe deeply into the part where you feel pain.

TIME MANAGEMENT

◆

Time can play nasty tricks on you, and the way you view and manage your time can often lead to unwanted emotions. Fortunately, there are simple mindful techniques to change your mindset.

LIFE AS A STUDENT IS FAR LESS STRUCTURED than it was at school, which can come as a shock – especially if you are used to having your day timetabled, meals and transport organized, and work prioritized for you. You may feel that you never have enough time – there is so much to do and not enough time to do it. Your mind may drift to the dark side of pessimistic worries: 'I will never get this done' or 'I just can't do it' or 'I'm never going to pass'. On the other hand, when the summer holidays arrive, you may envisage endless days spent soaking up the sun and enjoying non-stop social arrangements. Yet in reality, you find that having so much time has sucked you into a void of boredom, loneliness and frustration.

Absurd as it may sound, stop. Take a pause from your work, turn off the laptop and silence your phone

However you feel about time, try to challenge your relationship with this ticking friend or foe. Absurd as it may sound, stop. Take a pause from your work, turn off the laptop and silence your phone.

Asking you to stop and do 'nothing' might sound strange, especially when you feel that everything needs to be completed or feel so sick with loneliness that you want time to swallow you up. How is doing nothing going to help? Even if we find a moment of stillness – it could just be stopping and focusing on your breath for three counts – in that moment, time is boundless and infinite. There is just the here and now.

While you pause, you may feel a momentary feeling of peace. Try to draw on that inner sensation of tranquillity when you approach the next task in your never-ending to-do list or consider how to alleviate the boredom that is suffocating you.

Mindful Tips for Time Management

- There is only the now – don't put off what could be achieved in this very moment.
- You may be physically ready to work, sitting with all your materials at your table, but mentally absent. Be aware that your focus has shifted and ground yourself back in the present moment by taking a few slow and steady breaths.
- Don't fret about what you haven't done yet. Instead be fully absorbed in your current task.

If you are fully in the zone when you work and do not let your mind drift to your worries, you will be able to absorb more information, your concentration will improve and you can answer your questions with precision.

The more you practise moment-to-moment awareness, the more you will begin to notice that your thoughts and anxieties are not you. You do not have to be ruled by your internal monologue. Like the moment of calmness that came and then quickly passed when you stopped what you were doing, your thoughts, stresses, anxieties and worries will also subside. It may feel that they won't go away, and you may want to throw this book across the room, but keep trying. If you can be fully present even just for brief pockets of the day, then eventually you will learn to watch your worries float away into nothingness while your inner calmness and focus remain strong.

Visualizations for
Detaching from Your Thoughts

- Imagine thoughts are like carriages on a train that are constantly moving forward.
- Imagine each thought as part of an old-fashioned movie reel; a picture is quickly shown and then wound on.
- Imagine thoughts as clouds in the sky that drift on by.

Let Thoughts Drift On By

You might feel that your flow of thoughts could prevent you from being fully present. Here I give further suggestions on how you can learn to befriend your thinking. Just as knowing how to focus on your breath is vital to mindfulness, so is how to process and deal with your thoughts.

To see thoughts as old movie reels or scenes in the theatre gives you the ability to watch thoughts enter and exit as on the screen or stage. You can begin to witness thoughts as moving moments and realize that thoughts are not pure truths. If you can apply this or a similar visualization (see facing page) during times of negativity, self-criticism and low self-esteem, you are more likely to change the way you relate to your thoughts. Instead of becoming caught up in them, you become a spectator.

CHAPTER TWO

FOOD FOR THOUGHT

Mindful eating is about noticing the taste, texture and smell of your food and being fully aware of how your body responds to the sensations and satisfaction of eating. It is not about sitting in isolated silence but rather the focus is on being conscious of your surroundings and attentively listening, laughing and responding while sharing a meal with friends or family. Choosing to eat mindfully might also mean turning off your computer or phone so that you can enjoy your food wholeheartedly.

THE ACT OF EATING

Living in a world where there is often such a cultural and social emphasis on beauty and body image, you may be preoccupied with what you eat. However, how much attention do you ever pay to how you eat? Do you savour your food? Eat slowly and consciously? Although you may be concerned about your waistline and your food intake, the act of eating is usually done without thought.

I T IS NOT SURPRISING MANY PEOPLE are unhappy with their bodies given the artificially filtered and Photoshopped models appearing on social media sites, magazines, posters and TV. Even those who are a healthy size can feel inadequate and ugly when they compare themselves to an unrealistic image. For some young adults, food can become an issue rather than a pleasure. If you are able to approach eating and your diet with self-compassion, this everyday activity can bring you joy and self-appreciation.

Having a healthy and balanced diet has a positive impact on your concentration, confidence, sleeping habits, energy levels and overall mental attitude. Being aware of which foods are good for you and making a conscious effort to eat well can improve your life greatly. That said, the aim of mindful eating is not about following fad diets, restricting what you eat or striving for a certain weight. Rather, it is about eating what you like – indulge or eat healthily, but do so with full awareness.

When we eat with complete attentiveness, we are able to value each meal, eat in moderation and find a moment of peace each time we tuck into our food. If you can be in tune with what your body wants and needs rather than responding to the little voice in your head pleading for that extra chocolate bar, you are more likely to eat when you are hungry, stop when you are full and not turn to food as a form of escape.

What Affects Our Eating Habits?

Several factors influence what, how and when we choose to eat and these, in turn, affect our ability to digest our food.

Emotions

Your emotions have a huge influence on your relationship with food. For example, if you are feeling sad or lonely, you may want to eat or overeat to fill your emptiness. You might hardly eat at all when feeling emotionally stuck and confused. Sometimes, eating can be a way to divert attention from what you are really feeling. It is easier and more pleasurable to finish a tub of ice cream or a box of chocolates than to confront your emotional pain. If you eat for emotional reasons, you often do so without consideration, but once you have overindulged, you might feel regretful and annoyed with yourself. Learning to recognize emotional eating habits can improve your daily nutrition, and with an improved diet you are likely to feel better about yourself.

Stress

When frazzled with work, it is very easy to wolf down food without thought. Equally your mind might urge you to go and grab a snack as a cunning way to procrastinate. This urge also comes from the fact that stress releases the hormone cortisol, which can lead to food cravings and have a negative effect on how you digest food.

Tiredness

The more tired you are the more you tend to eat. You may find you have so many assignments that you stay up until all hours to cram it all in. However, by working with an exhausted head you are not only forfeiting your concentration but also a healthy diet. It is when you are sleep deprived that you crave foods high in fat and sugars to keep you going. This unwholesome regime can lead to weight gain, which can affect your self-esteem and confidence.

Finance

As a student you may be short of money. It requires good organization and careful planning to eat well on a tight budget, such as finding out the times when the supermarkets reduce the prices of fresh produce and buying cheap staples in bulk. Otherwise you may end up buying unhealthy and more expensive supplies by making last-minute trips to more expensive local stores.

Eating with Intention

My eating habits were once unhealthy. It wasn't until I started to practise mindful meditations that I woke up to how my eating behaviour was affecting me physically and mentally.

When I was 21, I studied abroad for a term in Amsterdam. During this time I suffered from chronic stomach aches. I remember one night I had arranged to go to a club with friends. But I couldn't leave the house because I was in so much pain. My stomach was in spasms and I was enduring waves of intolerable discomfort. Admittedly, at the time I was more concerned with the fact that I was going to miss out than the pain.

> *I didn't want to waste valuable study time, so when I was peckish I would go to the kitchen and quickly nibble on some cereal*

In hindsight, I did not have healthy eating habits. I didn't want to waste valuable study time, so when I was peckish I would go to the kitchen and quickly nibble on some cereal straight from the box. This habit earned me the name of 'nibbler' when I was at university. I ate only because I had to, I didn't cook much and I didn't cook well.

My awful stomach aches continued into my mid-twenties. I thought that I must have Irritable Bowel Syndrome (IBS) but when I went to see doctors, they did not confirm this.

It was not until one of my sisters pointed out that my on-going stomach aches could be related to my emotional state that I began to contemplate this. She asked me whether I was stressed or upset. I didn't feel particularly stressed, but on reflection, the pains always came around the time I had important exams or deadlines. I would work for hours and thought that I was coping fine mentally. But physically, my body was telling me to stop and calm down. By nibbling, and rushing my food, I was making myself ill. What's more, I was downplaying my stress levels because I wanted to be seen as a bright and able student.

When I first started practising mindfulness meditation, I realized how dreadful my eating habits had become. I would automatically grab food and, before I knew it, what was in my hand had rapidly been devoured. When I first did the chocolate exercise (see facing page), I thought to myself, 'When do I ever really taste, smell and touch my food?' Now, I make a conscious effort to acknowledge my emotional state before I eat. If I am feeling frantic, preoccupied, anxious or worried, instead of shoving the first thing that comes to hand into my mouth, I take a few moments to focus on my breath and the sights and sounds around me. Simply bringing myself back to the present moment enables me to eat my food with calm appreciation. I also find eating with intention also helps with my stomach problems and relaxes my body and mind. Eating is always a pleasure.

CHOCOLATE EXERCISE
THREE MINUTES

A little treat can be tempting when you want to be temporarily transported away from the challenges of your studies. This meditation will take you on a journey that will hopefully resonate with you at mealtimes. You can apply the suggestions to any food you enjoy.

- Take a small square of chocolate and resist the urge to eat it straight away.
- Hold the chocolate in your hand and note the texture against your skin.
- Can you bring awareness to its smoothness? Perhaps it is sticky against your palm.
- How are you holding the chocolate? Are you pinching it with your fingers or is it flat on the palm of your hand?
- Look at it as if for the first time. Notice its shape, colour and size.
- Bring the chocolate to your nose and smell it. What do you notice? Does the smell bring back any memories or does it tempt you to eat it?
- Take a lick. What can you taste? Have you started to salivate? What is the first thing you notice?
- When you are ready, slowly put the chocolate in your mouth and resist the urge to gulp it down or chew.
- Feel the texture against the wall of your mouth, the weight on your tongue and the pressure on your teeth.
- Once you have played around with the sensations of the chocolate in your mouth, slowly begin to chew and swallow.
- What sounds can you hear? How does it move around your mouth and then slide down your throat?
- How do you feel once it is gone? Are you satisfied or do you want more?

We don't always have the time to pay such close attention to every bite of food. Nevertheless, if you try to approach all meals and snacks with intention rather than consuming your food mindlessly, this can help you bring greater gratification to the act of eating.

FOOD SHOPPING

◆

Mindful eating begins with mindful food shopping, whether it is done online, in your local grocery store or at a supermarket. The way we shop affects the global environment and if you learn to shop with consciousness, you help to make the world a healthier place.

WHEN YOU START UNIVERSITY, it might be the first time you are in complete control of doing your own food shop. You will probably find you are busy with other priorities, and shopping may feel like a chore, especially if you are feeling low, sluggish or stressed. Try to make food shopping a positive experience; it can be a welcome break from your studies and a good opportunity to implement mindfulness on regular basis.

Being mindful while you shop can make the everyday act of shopping a more interesting experience. As you browse the aisles, notice how your feet move across the floor and the noises you can hear. Focus on the array of colours, smells and textures of the foods on display. Be in the moment as you choose your items and be aware if you are shopping with your eyes or your stomach.

Mindful shopping doesn't just have to be about the physical act of buying products – the feel, look and smell of the food. You can also choose to be an environmentally conscientious shopper. The choices we make when we shop have a huge

global impact. Knowing how food is produced and where it is farmed helps you to make choices that are in line with your principles, opting for free-range eggs, for example. Equally, choosing unpackaged vegetables or foods with eco-friendly and recyclable packaging means that your shopping decisions can have a beneficial effect on the environment.

Tips for Eco-friendly Shopping

- Bring your own bags so you don't need to buy any plastic ones. You can also reuse plastic bags from home for bagging up fresh produce.
- Invest in a reusable water bottle and coffee cup.
- When possible, buy produce from local farmers.
- Try to buy fruit and vegetables that are in season and not air-freighted from far away. They will often be cheaper and have a lower carbon footprint.
- If you eat meat, try to buy free-range chicken and grass-fed lamb or beef.
- Be mindful of how food is packaged and ideally opt for reusable packaging or choose to buy items that are not prepacked.
- Avoid food waste. Plan the food you are going to buy, use leftovers to make another meal or share food with friends.

COOKING

◆

Mindfulness is at its most influential and effective when we let it seep into our daily lives. Turning the task of food preparation into a mindful experience can be easy and enjoyable.

FOR AMATEUR CHEFS FINDING THEIR FEET among the debris of dirty plates and saucers left by housemates, engaging in a mindful act of cooking may seem like an impossible task. Similarly, with a mountain of work that needs completing by an imminent deadline, cooking may even seem like an indulgent luxury. Yet one of the best ways to clear your mind is to remove yourself from your overflowing desk and do something that can spark all your senses. Apart from the nourishing end result, after cooking you will return to your studies refreshed.

The more you enjoy the art of cooking, the more skilful you become. By making mindful cooking part of your daily routine, you are likely to gain a new zest for food

If you can capture the sound of a sizzling onion as it hits the saucepan and the distinct aroma that lingers in the air with full awareness, the mundane task of frying a vegetable can turn into something tantalizing. If you can cook completely in the zone, you will truly appreciate the variety of colours, textures, tastes and sounds that cooking has to

offer. The more you enjoy the art of cooking, the more skilful you will become. By making mindful cooking part of your daily routine, you are likely to gain a new zest for food.

To be mindful when you cook, start by dedicating this time only to the act of cooking. Tell yourself that you won't be distracted by your phone, worrying about all the work you have to do or thinking about what you're going to wear on Saturday night.

Begin by laying out your ingredients on the kitchen worktop and notice the different colours in front of you. The more colourful your food, the more nutritious your meal will be. You could choose green, yellow and red vegetables, such as broccoli, sweetcorn and a red pepper; protein, for example, white chicken, fish or haricot beans, and a healthy carb, such as sweet potato or cauliflower.

As you begin chopping, commit your focus to the task. Place your food in the pan, on the hob or oven tray with precision and care. Listen to the sound as the hot oil begins to hiss and spit or the oven's fan starts to swirl energetically. Breathe in the smells that waft around the room and notice how they change in intensity as time passes.

Take little tastes as you are cooking and feel how the food moves and melts around your mouth. Relish the flavours and be attentive to what might be missing. Add extra seasoning bit by bit, noticing how this too can change the colour and taste of your dish.

As you serve your meal on the plate, be proud of your efforts and how all the elements of cooking have come together to make something wholesome. Before you begin to eat, bring attention to your breathing and then slowly indulge in your appetizing accomplishment.

Tips for Mindful Cooking

If cooking makes you feel frazzled, here are a few tips to help you remain completely in the zone.

* Consciously dedicate time to cooking.

* Bring your awareness to the colours, textures and smells of the food.

* While your food is sizzling, frying or baking, stay in the moment by watching it jump, rise, soften or crisp.

* Try not to shove your food in the oven, microwave or on the hob and then think 'job done'. Stay on the cooking journey for as long as possible.

SHARING FOOD

◆

Sharing a meal with housemates, friends or family provides an ideal opportunity to share stories, worries or hopes. By sharing your thoughts and feelings as well as the food on the table, you may find that you are not alone in the challenges you face.

SHARING FOOD IS A BASIC ELEMENT of cultures around the world and allows for a sense of belonging. By cooking and eating with your housemates or peers you can feel part of a community. Eating together mindfully can help you to become more in tune with those in different circumstances, more aware of others' sufferings or aspirations and more open-minded and respectful of other dietary requirements and traditions. You can choose to be totally present in this communal experience, thoughtfully enjoying the company.

Mealtimes can be an opportunity to bond with housemates or support them after a stressful day. You'll learn to get along, even if you don't become firm friends. Communal eating also provides a chance to watch out for other students' signs of depression or other mental-health issues. You may notice if anyone is drinking alcohol to excess or is increasingly withdrawn. Likewise, this could be a chance to air differences or to work through household issues. You may even find that this communal act encourages you to unwind and brings some light-hearted relief after a long day.

Eating with others also helps to highlight and improve your own eating habits. You are more likely to realize if you eat too fast when you notice that you have finished whereas those around you have barely made a dent in their meal. Messy eating habits are highlighted – in company, you will be more aware if tomato ketchup is lodged on the corner of your mouth or has made a bright splatter on your top. You may deliberately chew your food with your mouth closed. When food is shared, you might be conscious not to greedily grab a large portion as you can see how much there is to go round.

If you become more aware of your own eating habits in the company of others, then you can also apply this state of attention when you are eating on your own. Bring awareness to how you feel during and after your meal; knowing when you have had enough is key to mindful eating. If you eat in a rush or in an agitated state, you run the risk of overeating and getting a stomach ache. The signals to your brain that tell you your stomach is full become fuzzy and blurred because your mind is transfixed on other matters.

Typically, it takes approximately 20 minutes from when you start to eat before your stomach sends a message to your brain indicating that you are full. If you take your time over your food, you are less likely to overeat because you have listened to the hints from your body. Implementing mindful eating helps you to eat less without going on a diet and could mean you spend less on food.

DRINKING MEDITATION
THREE MINUTES

Drinking can often be a mindless act. Whether it's swigging your water once you realize how dehydrated you are or downing your coffee in the morning to perk you up, you often don't notice all the sips, swigs and gulps that happen in a day. Yet if you give this regular activity a moment of clear and conscious attention, you will have several opportunities every day to gain a sense of grounding and stillness. Try this drinking meditation.

• Once you have your drink in your hand, take a moment to feel the sensation of the glass, ceramic or plastic in your hand. Does it feel cold or hot? What is the shape of the glass, bottle or mug? Take time to acknowledge the texture of the object holding your drink.

• Does your drink have a distinctive smell? If so, does this evoke any memories or feelings?

• Be attentive to the movement of bringing the drink to your mouth. How are you holding the cup or bottle? Are you grasping it or holding it with a loose grip.

• Taste the drink swirling in your mouth. Don't rush to swallow too fast.

• Feel the sensation as the drink glides down your throat then reaches your belly. How does this make you feel?

• Is the drink quenching your thirst, or if it is hot, can you feel it warming your throat and belly?

CHAPTER THREE

SWITCHING OFF

*In order to switch off mentally, it is vital
to plan some time out, away from technological
devices and the virtual world. If technology can be
used mindfully or put aside for brief periods, you
can benefit from the ripple effect of a digital detox.
Your sleeping habits improve, you achieve a clearer,
calmer mindset, and you can feel content in
the present moment.*

USING THE INTERNET PRODUCTIVELY

◆

The internet has had a transformative impact on the world. On one level, it can inspire, motivate, connect and teach. Yet being too dependent on the online world can lead to addictive behaviour, unhappiness, anxiety and a decline in self-worth. It's possible to find a balance and use the internet productively and healthily.

The Need to be Online

As our dependence on technology expands, it is impossible to withdraw from the virtual world. Universities and workplaces communicate with us online so to remove yourself completely is not feasible. You can delete your social media accounts, but if all other students are using technology to connect and make social arrangements, withdrawing from social media could hinder your opportunities to make new friends. If we are able to use technology mindfully, we can begin to have a healthier relationship with it.

Are You Addicted?

First, notice your own habits when using technology. Our mood is often affected by messages we've read or posts we've seen. Do you feel rewarded when you receive a 'like' for a selfie, group photo or written post? Perhaps you feel a sense of satisfaction if you look at your phone and are greeted with a message or comment that helps suggest that you are liked.

The pleasure we experience when we receive praise online can be likened to the happiness we feel when we complete a task or the satisfaction of achieving a personal goal. The use of the internet can similarly trigger the release of dopamine in the brain, a hormone that can make you feel good about yourself (see page 20). The pleasure we get when we engage

---

Give Yourself a Break

Taking short breaks away from your phone can help you to achieve a sense of calmness, composure and stability. Here are a few ideas:

• Leave your phone at home and walk to your local shops.

• Place your phone in a different room while you watch a TV programme or film.

• Have one meal a day without checking your phone.

• Give yourself a set time away from checking your devices by setting a timer. You could start with three minutes and work up to 15 minutes.

Notice how you feel when you choose to step away from your devices. Do you feel agitated or nervous? Perhaps you welcome this temporary respite. Whatever you feel, remember not to judge yourself. If at first you find the experience unsettling, don't give up.

---

online can trigger obsessive behaviour. We may constantly check messages, feel disconnected if we are not gaming, or out of touch if we are not reading and responding immediately to news and posts.

Being aware that you have reached for your phone five times in the space of ten minutes can help you to understand that you might be more attached to your phone than you had thought. Equally, just as we can feel validation and pleasure when we are online, we can also feel a surge of negative emotions ranging from rejection, to jealousy, loneliness, fear and confusion. Becoming less committed to your online presence may give you relief from the pressures that exist in the virtual world and in real life.

Use Technology Mindfully

Often we are so consumed with our internet use that we sacrifice the natural rhythm of our breath. If we are totally absorbed in what we are reading, writing or posting, we may hold our breath or breathe shallowly. This can happen when we are giving our full concentration to anything. But if we are restricting our breath, we are restricting our minds and bodies. We begin to feel tense, with clenched jaws, tight shoulders and poor posture.

Likewise, by stopping the flow of our breath we may be stopping the flow of our creativity or closing our minds, giving us a narrow and limited perception of what we are looking at online. Focusing on how you breathe as you tap or scroll will help you to feel more relaxed and will affect how you choose to respond and communicate. You could dedicate your first five minutes in the online realm to being mindful: pay attention to how you breathe, the sounds in the room and how you feel physically.

We can also take advantage of the mindful movement that flourishes online. There are numerous podcasts dedicated to meditating and encouraging us to step out of our heads. If I have trouble falling asleep, I listen to a mindful meditation for sleep online, which helps me to relax. Once you see how much is out there to help people who struggle with winding down, you can be reassured that you are not alone with your overactive mind or sleep problems.

RECHARGING

You may or may not be an internet junkie. If you are, you may find that the desire to enter this computer-generated domain often occurs at night when you are cosy in bed. Making the decision to free your-self from the virtual world before you drift off will allow you to sleep better and work more effectively the following day.

I F WE ARE CONSTANTLY GLUED to our phones with an urge to know instantaneously who's done what, to respond, to upload, to write a meaningful post, our fingers tapping away, we are tuning out of our sense of self. With an attachment to an artificial environment that is hooked on appearance, positive perceptions and numerous opinions, it is not surprising that we worry about the judgement of others. Being online can be tiring and all-consuming.

With bright screens buzzing and everything a simple click or swipe away, it's so easy to have our eyes fixated downwards and to detach ourselves from the here and now. Even at night our phones are there, close to our faces and blocking out what we feel in the present moment. It is normal to feel jealous, overwhelmed and overtired when we are constantly looking at past events and future goals. If we just take a moment to stop, put our phones down and focus on the simple inhalation and exhalation of our breath, momentarily our racing thoughts are silenced and the world that seems so vast seems slightly closer.

Although we are aware that bed is supposed to be the place for peace and serenity, it is here our minds often feel most active. Knowing that if we sleep well, we feel well doesn't necessarily mean we are able to use this insight when our heads hit the pillow.

Try switching off all your devices and practise this 20-minute mindful mediation at night so you can learn to wind down and experience a good night's sleep. Before you start, ensure that you are comfortable in your bed, lying on your back with your legs and arms uncrossed, palms facing downwards.

MINDFUL EXERCISE

BODY-SCAN MEDITATION
20 MINUTES

- Feel the weight of your body sinking comfortably into your mattress.
- Bring your attention to your breathing, observing your inhalation and exhalation.
- You will now move through each body part, breathing into it. Be aware of any sensations, such as aches or tingles, and accept them. It doesn't matter if you don't notice anything at all.
- Bring your attention to your big toes. Move your attention to each other toe and then to your feet.
- Focus on the lower part of your legs, your knees and thighs.
- Become aware of your pelvis, hips and buttocks and the organs in between. Imagine you are filling these parts with replenishing oxygen.
- Move to the stomach and lower back. Feel the contact of your lower back on the mattress.
- Take a few moments to notice the sensation in your stomach as you breathe in and out, feeling it expand and deflate.
- Bring your attention to your chest and upper back.
- Focus on both arms. Become aware of the palms, then your fingertips. Move this awareness up your arms to your shoulders.
- Focus on your neck. Is there tension here? Feel the back of the neck relax into your pillow.
- Move your attention to your jaw, noticing if it's clenched. Part your lips slightly. Feel your tongue resting in your mouth.
- Pay attention to the back of your head, letting it feel heavy on your pillow.
- Bring your awareness to the top of your head. Imagine all the tension in your head draining down through your body into the ground.
- Focus on your whole body, breathing for a few minutes.
- Think to yourself: my entire body is now comfortable and relaxed. With your mind focused on your breath and body, use this sense of stillness to drift off into peaceful sleep.

Removing Myself from Social Media

I considered my social media use to be normal. While watching TV, waiting for someone or feeling slightly bored, I would scroll my newsfeed on social media. I might like a picture of a close friend or yearn to be on the tropical island that an acquaintance was visiting. I would look with aimless affection, not really caring what was posted but still unable to remove my scrolling finger and wandering eyes.

Often, I would find myself online and it would be around ten minutes before I realized that I had been an active participant on my sites. My mind and body seemed to operate on autopilot: pick up phone, check phone, purposelessly absorb other people's lives, put down phone, feel slightly agitated (not fully sure why) then repeat the process 15 minutes later. I knew it was pointless and each time I did it, I reprimanded myself: 'Why you are spending so much time online?' 'Get off it – what you are doing?' Yet the compulsion continued.

The trouble with social media sites is that they are bursting with fake news. Most people seem to be happy, attractive, fulfilled and living life to the full. We rarely receive an honest glimpse into the loneliness, heartache, pain and true suffering of life. We may occasionally read a morbid post but overall people want to show off online and accept an ego boost from the filtered pictures and comments.

Admittedly, I wasn't ever an avid photo pusher, but if I was going to an upload an image of myself I made sure I looked eye-catching, slender and content. Most of the pictures displayed me on holiday, sunning it up with a cocktail in hand and a smile from ear to ear. I wasn't one to post a bed-head, early-morning, grumpy shot with a caption, 'coffee most needed'. I showed the world the best aspects of my life and I felt a sense of triumph when I received numerous likes or a complimentary comment. However, my online attachment changed when my best friend was thrown a massive curve ball.

When my friend was in hospital with a life-threatening illness, I no longer had any wish to read, write, post, comment or browse my social media networks. I was finding it hard to connect and function in the real world, let alone a world that glowed with untouchable, blissful lives. It didn't seem fair that my friend, who is so innocent, considerate and kind, could be struck with such misfortune. I felt annoyed, envious and resentful when I saw posts of other people having nights out. It felt like a constant reminder of how life should be and how far from me it was. I decided it would be best to remove myself from social media.

A year later, my friend is better and we are no longer drained by days spent in hospital. Still, I remain absent online. If I were to reconnect, I would no longer feel a surge of comparison, jealousy or distress, or an obligation to keep up with my virtual 'friends'. I no longer obsessively and pointlessly roam online, and this allows me to feel more connected in the present moment.

Morning Mindfulness

Avoiding the rush to our devices as soon as our eyes open can help us feel more refreshed and stop us from feeling dazed before the day has even started. Take a moment to be present, and to recognize what you are thinking and feeling. It can help you achieve a stronger sense of self and a calmer outlook.

MINDFUL EXERCISE

A MEDITATION TO START THE DAY
THREE MINUTES

A short, achievable meditation to start every morning can have a positive impact on how you feel and focus for the rest of the day.

• Slowly open your eyes as you wake up.

• Make a conscious effort not to rush to your phone or to rise too quickly out of bed.

• Notice how your body feels lying on your mattress. Stay in this position for a moment, appreciating the comfort and security of your bed.

• Begin to pay attention to the gentle rise and fall of your breath.

• Notice the morning light in your room and listen to any surrounding noises.

• Take a moment to stretch your body from head to toe.

• Slowly rise to a seated position and for a moment, focus your attention on sitting and breathing.

• With this calm, slow and mindful wakening, you should set the intention to continue the day in this manner – moving, thinking and acting with consideration of yourself and others.

When you wake up, pay attention to the flow of your breath and the sights and sounds in and around your room.

Stretch with full intention and smile for a few seconds. Starting the day with a smile (even if you have to force yourself) can help you adopt an optimistic attitude.

If and when you reach for your device, use the opportunity for a moment of mindfulness. Try tapping in your passwords with complete deliberation or focusing on the rhythm of your breath as you read your messages, daily news or feeds.

IMPROVING FOCUS

It's hard not to procrastinate with your rectangular friend vibrating on the table. It may be tempting to go for an immediate hit of online gaming or Snapchatting rather than face up to the pressures of your workload. But clearing your mind and improving your focus might be easier than you think.

To be mindful is to be aware of thoughts and feelings, noticing that they come and go like the carriages of a moving train. Taking a moment to acknowledge and accept what you are thinking and feeling rather than deferring your attention to a screen has been proven to help with focus and clarity of mind. If you are fully aware in the present moment, the temptation to be distracted will decrease, and with a more focused mentality your ability to study and to make decisions can be drastically improved. Allow yourself a few moments in which to feel anchored in the present moment and you will be better able to absorb and understand the information needed for your studies.

Focus doesn't always have to be about the attention given to academic work, but also the focus we give to our friends, family and even ourselves. How many meals have you had with those close to you, only to find that within minutes the phones are out? You are no longer making eye contact, but your heads are down and those at the dinner table are no longer there but are engrossed in their own virtual worlds.

It's fascinating how quickly we can be collectively transported away from our present company. Sometimes it can be like a Mexican wave of technological use; once one person gets out their gadget, everyone follows suit. The unified decision not to talk may feel briefly comfortable, but in the long term, we are losing opportunities to form meaningful and strong bonds. Perhaps next time you meet a friend for a coffee or have a family meal, make a joint decision to put phones to one side, to talk and to give full attention to listening – or even at points to sit in silence, without the distraction of your digital companions.

MINDFUL EXERCISE

AVOIDING DISTRACTIONS
FIVE MINUTES

We can concentrate for only approximately 20 minutes at a time, so, when you are studying, give your eyes and brain a break every 20 minutes, by looking away from your computer or book. Bring your attention to the sensation of breathing for a few minutes and you will feel refreshed. If you are using a device, move away from it or put it on sleep.

● Wherever you are sitting to study, take a moment to recognize how your body feels. Can you feel the sensation of your buttocks on your chair or mattress? Is your back hurting you? Are you slouching or sitting up straight?

● Acknowledge your body in the room where you are working and make a conscious effort to straighten your back.

● Feel the soles of your feet on the floor – move to the side of your bed if you are sitting on the bed. Let yourself feel anchored by the ground beneath you.

● For a moment, try to forget about your work and simply focus on your inhalation and exhalation.

● Take a moment to acknowledge any stress, and when a thought comes to mind, label it for what it is: worry, doubt, irritation, fear, etc. Once you have recognized and labelled your thought, let it pass on by.

● Try to bring your attention back to the sensation of breathing. Let the focus on your breath begin to calm your thoughts.

● After a few minutes of mindful breathing, take a moment to notice the smells and noises in and around your room.

● Take a deep inhale and exhale. Then return to work.

CHAPTER FOUR

TUNING IN

*If you can listen to others with
undivided attention, you can expand your
ability to empathize, connect on a deeper level
and be content in the moment. Mindfully listening
requires absorbing what someone else is saying without
an ulterior motive. Listening to others, to sounds
around you and to your own internal voice requires
deliberate concentration, but once you have tuned
into the art of listening, you will become more
open-minded, non-judgemental and able to
cope with conflicting opinions.*

LISTENING

◆

Hearing is an involuntary act that involves recognizing sounds through vibrations in the ear. Listening requires an active decision to receive, interpret, infer and take in what someone else is saying. It also requires attentiveness, which in turn leads to understanding and compassion.

OUR MINDS ARE OFTEN BUZZING with a multitude of thoughts and it is not easy to turn these off when someone else is talking. How often do you find yourself mid-conversation, seeing the other person's mouth move and hearing their vocal sounds, but not really being engaged in what they are saying? Your mind might be focusing on past events or future situations, or caught up in a completely random thought. It is not unusual to pre-empt a response or to think about another 'more interesting' topic to interject with. During one conversation, there can often be two very different discussions occurring. Neither person is really listening or sharing, so there is no genuine bonding.

Although you may be living in a bustling house, if you are not listening to others or feel that others are not listening to you, you may start to feel lonely and not valued. If you find that your mind has wandered during a conversation, try to acknowledge this and gently bring your attention back to the subject at hand. Making the decision to listen actively to another person allows that individual to open up, and the barriers between you can begin to come down. They might reciprocate and be attentive to you too, fostering an exchange of compassion and thoughtfulness.

By bringing consciousness to the manner in which we listen, we are able to stay open to the viewpoint of those who are speaking and to recognize personal judgements as they enter our minds. When someone is talking, we may find that we are automatically becoming defensive and critical. At this point, we stop listening completely and we are already more concerned with our internal voice, which we deem to be the right one. In contrast, the intention of listening mindfully is to focus on what the speaker is saying without the need to interject with a personal comment.

If you notice that your inner opinion has overridden someone else's and that you are no longer listening to what they have to say, consciously bring your focus back to the present conversation by focusing on your breath, what you can sense around you, and the words and gestures of the person talking. Taking this one step further, you could even try bringing your attention to the rhythm of the speaker's breath and try to breathe at the same time and pace. This also brings you back to the present moment and makes you feel more deeply connected. Using these listening techniques, you may find the person speaking has something useful to say, even if you don't agree with it.

Listening can also apply to what is not said, an awareness of silence or the emptiness of words that can hide someone's misery or suffering. University life can be really hard, and people may withdraw or hide behind a mask of false happiness. If someone is talking and you can listen and notice the subtleties of communication, you can begin to understand what they are really feeling. How many times have you been asked how you are and then replied with a standard 'I'm OK' — when really you feel down or stressed? When you ask this question, pay attention to the tone of the reply and watch the responses of the person's eyes, hands or posture. Thes may provide clues about any issues the individual might be facing. To truly understand the answer to this simple question, we need to have a willingness to listen to what is being said, often between the lines, and a desire to try to help or comfort a friend or acquaintance who is feeling off balance.

Listening Skills for Success

Active listening skills are essential for success at university, from listening to lectures, to participating in seminar groups and presentations by your peers. Listening carefully, asking perceptive questions and giving constructive feedback to peers will assist your learning and help you to retain information.

Practising Mindful Listening

When we really listen to someone, we are offering that person security and trust. You can picture this by imagining you are securely holding that person's feeling or thoughts so that they can openly express want they may find hard to share. We allow the person speaking to feel respected, comfortable and at ease. For some, this deep level of listening comes naturally. For others, it may be a skill they need to work on and improve. The following tips can help:

• Make an effort to tune out any distractions during and before a conversation. Put your phone on silent, stop work or shut your laptop. Tell yourself that for the next few minutes, you will keep your mind focused on the person talking.

• Make it clear that you are physically and mentally present by making eye contact with the speaker and having open arms and posture. This way, the person speaking is less likely to feel criticized or ignored.

• Be aware of how you respond physically to a comment. Knowing when you have changed your physical position or facial expression can make you more thoughtful with your verbal response.

• Acknowledge the body language and expressions of the speaker. Is what they are saying in line with their physical message? Perhaps you can listen to what they are really feeling by bringing awareness to the tone, intonation, pace, pitch and volume of their voice, and any pauses.

- Recognize if your mind is getting carried away with your own thoughts. Gently and non-judgementally acknowledge this and return your attention to what the speaker is saying.
- Try to put yourself in the other person's position by listening with an open mind and heart.

DEALING WITH CONFRONTATION

As you move through life, there will always be people who antagonize you. You may find yourself sharing a home with students you clash with or mixing with people with different political views. You will be dealing with figures in authority at university or maybe working in a job at the bottom of the food chain.

LEARNING TO COPE WITH THE TRIALS and tribulations of all sorts of relationships will help you to achieve a more stable, balanced and contented life. During conflict we usually want to protect ourselves from being hurt or emotionally vulnerable. As a result, we try to control our emotions and instead can respond with blame, fear or judgement. And so begins a two-way battle to be stronger, more resilient and fierce. Alternatively, if we paused and focused on our raw physical sensations and our ability to be vulnerable, our own response might not be so volatile. When you find yourself getting into a heated argument, try tuning into how you respond physically. Focusing on the sensations that you feel can help to settle your mind, and your approach to the confrontation may become more level headed.

Often, if somebody makes us angry and we try to express our feelings, our opinions are lost in our heightened manner of speech – which can make an acceptable point sound invalid. When you feel impassioned, the best thing to do is to take a few deep breaths before you talk. It is also helpful to recognize the sensations in your body that are being provoked by your emotion, such as sweaty palms, a rapid heartbeat or tension in the shoulders. If you notice you are clenching your fists or pursing your lips, relaxing these physical tensions may help to decrease your anger. Try to tell yourself that you accept your emotional state because what you accept, you can eventually let go. It is when we become carried away with our emotions that they become harder to unchain.

If you are finding it hard to turn inwards, try to notice the other person's physical responses. Has their breathing become heavier? Are they clenching their jaws or grinding their teeth? Being able to divert your attention to what is physically happening is a particularly useful skill if you find yourself in a position of confrontation with someone in authority, such as a lecturer, tutor or employer. Shifting your focus to the other person's physical reactions may enable you to hold back an impromptu response that could land you in further trouble. Even in the most pressing situations, mindfulness can help to ease and calm explosive emotions.

EXPRESSING YOURSELF

◆

As well as listening skills, the ability to express yourself is key to any successful relationship. Sometimes, you may have disagreements and these need to be aired in a mindful instead of a confrontational way.

Sometimes I can be really confident, bubbly and comfortable in social situations. At other times I am an introvert, struggling to find words that will fit into a conversation, desperate to be on my own and so shy that I turn ruby red the minute I'm under the spotlight. When I was younger, I used to hide behind my mother's legs if I was introduced to a new person and hated to attend group activities. As I grew up, this inhibition decreased but I still found it difficult to communicate well.

I detest confrontation and I used to avoid it at all costs. As a result, things were left unspoken, which often only fuelled a conflict. What's more, I used to find it particularly hard to be vulnerable. In the early stages of my relationship with my partner, I struggled to express what I felt. It was difficult for me to reveal my true feelings of anger, love, frustration or jealousy. This meant that things that were bothering me were articulated in different ways; I would be passive-aggressive, sullen or retreat into myself. Over time, and with patience and understanding from my partner, my ability to express my feelings has developed.

Try to be aware of your communicative habits and mindful of how these could improve so that you can form better relationships with all those around you. There are some simple ways to do this. Make sure that you maintain eye contact with the person you are speaking to and have open body language – try not to cross your arms. This posture relays the message that you are willing and able to let someone into your confidence. While the person responds to you, smile and nod, and repeat or paraphrase what they say to confirm that you have taken it in.

Reaching Out

It can be especially difficult to communicate what you are feeling if you are depressed, anxious, lonely, stressed or are experiencing other unpleasant emotions. You may feel ashamed of how you feel, particularly as there is the added pressure to have a positive university experience. When older people remark that these will be the best years of your

If you think that your feelings are not normal, it can be hard to ask for help

life, it can make you feel worse. If you think that your feelings are not normal, it can be hard to ask for help. But you are not alone or having abnormal feelings; it is natural to be overwhelmed or weighed down by perplexing thoughts and feelings, so do not be afraid to reach out for support.

Here are a few suggestions when you need support:

• Ask to meet up with a friend for a coffee. If you talk to a friend far away, it's good to make it a video call so you can read each other's facial expressions.

• Learn to recognize the signs of when you are run down or feeling low and allow yourself a treat. With the pressures of study and life in general, it is easy to neglect the small pleasures that can make a big difference to your mind, body and soul. Listen to yourself and dedicate time to self-care in any way you find enjoyable.

• Attend a relaxing yoga class or go for a walk, swim or run – these activities help to improve your overall health.

• If you feel that you are overworking, make sure that you take regular short breaks during the day.

• Many people find it easier to repress emotions than to tackle them face on. If you are looking for an outlet for your thoughts and feelings, you could try expressing them in a diary, letter or email to yourself.

• Make use of internet helplines.

• All colleges and universities offer support for students under pressure, or you could speak to your GP for advice.

Reaching Out to Others

You may notice that a housemate or someone in your social or study group is suffering. You may not even know them well, but realize that they are in need of help. The way in which you reach out to someone who is in anguish can make a huge difference to their recovery. Offering to meet up for a chat in a non-threatening, comfortable environment can help the person to reveal their thoughts and feelings. If they are not ready to talk, let them know that you are there for them when they are ready and that you will not judge them. The person will know that their troubles have been noticed and that support is available.

When you talk to a friend who is having difficulties, they may seem emotionally stuck or unable to find the words to articulate their feelings. You may find it helpful to ask open-ended questions. Make sure that you finish the conversation positively, perhaps with a smile, a hug or a gentle squeeze of their arm. This way, hopefully your friend will feel acknowledged and understood.

These suggestions may sound obvious but it is tough when you are engaged in conversation with someone who is

The way in which you reach out to someone who is in anguish can make a huge difference to their recovery

suffering psychologically. You may desperately want to help but realize that nothing you say or do can make a difference. Even though it may feel as if nothing you do is of any benefit, just being there and letting the person know you want to listen can be a massive relief and support.

THOUGHTS & SOUNDS

◆

Mindful listening requires skilful attention to be fully present and focused on what is being said, and it allows you to become involved in a generous giving and receiving exchange. Yet when we apply this skill to our own thoughts, it can seem scary at first.

WHEN WE BEGIN TO LISTEN TO THE VOICES, murmurs, whispers and humming of our minds, we may notice that our thoughts are rapid, constantly changing and often arbitrary. What's more, when we become carried away with our thoughts we can enter a fantasy land, a state of ruminative negativity or restless worry. Listening to our thoughts as they come and go, and not giving them too much airtime in our minds gives us a grounded and stable mentality, and stops our thoughts from taking us on a dark and turbulent voyage. We need to train the mind to recognize that thoughts are not tangible facts. The first step is to listen to external sounds and see how we react to them.

Sounds of every spectrum float, infiltrate and glide around us, but many sounds escape our ears if we don't consciously tap into them. Take a moment just to stop and listen to the noises around you – it is enthralling how complex our surroundings are. Perhaps you can hear the faint cry of a siren, the background drone of music, bustle on the streets, the whooshing and beeping of cars or the low purr of the central heating system. When you're in a quiet space, you will detect faint sounds in the air. You may hear your own breath, the wind or the rustle of the leaves on a tree.

When we start to pay attention to sounds, we very quickly begin to attach emotions or stories to what we are hearing. Imagine you are in the library, keen to begin working, when the echoes of obnoxious chatter bombards your zone. Suddenly, the annoyance you feel overrides your ability to start your work. Or maybe you are in the cinema and the crunching of crisps takes your attention away from the action in the film. Negative thoughts then enter your mind: 'I knew I should never have come here to work' or 'How can people be so inconsiderate?' Once one negative thought pops up, it is not long before you embark on a heartfelt rant inside your head. Equally, you may hear a noise that triggers a positive memory or emotion and before you know it, you have been transported to your past or are daydreaming about your future. Much like thoughts, when we become attached to the sounds around us and start feeding them stories, we can become caught up in a flood of associations.

If you can learn to focus on sounds without linking what you hear to a narrative in your mind, then you can apply this skill to your thoughts. Our natural tendency is to reflect on a sound or form a reaction to it: 'I like it' or 'It's annoying'. The intention in a sound meditation is simply to listen, receive and notice. Try to register with curiosity that sounds come and go

SOUNDS MEDITATION
TEN MINUTES

The aim of this meditation to bring awareness to the significance we place on sounds. See if you can move towards recognizing sounds for their raw qualities – their pitch, tone, volume, duration and pattern – instead of labelling the sound or attaching a story to it. If you can notice that sounds appear, dissolve and change from moment to moment, you can realize this experience is similar to the nature of our thoughts.

• Begin by sitting comfortably, with a straight posture and feet firmly on the ground. Start to bring attention to the rhythm and flow of your breath.

• Once you feel settled, expand this attention to the sounds around you.

• Notice sounds as they arise, soften and melt away. Try not to search for certain sounds; instead, let sounds enter from all directions. Be open to the variety of sounds around you, not becoming fixating on one noise but moving with the change, pitch and pace of the different reverberations.

• Be aware of sounds as sounds, nothing more or less. Notice when you begin to label a sound, such as a voice, a passing car, a baby crying, TV, the kettle boiling or the clinking of cutlery. Once you realize that you are labelling the sounds, try to bring your attention back to the basic sensations of the sounds.

• If you find that you start thinking deeply about the sounds or that the sounds take you on a journey, try to bring your awareness back to the sensory nature of the sounds: the length, pitch, tone or volume. If you realize you have attached a meaning or a story to what you have heard, than gently and non-judgementally come back to your breath and try again to refocus on the raw quality of the sound.

• After focusing on the sounds, you can let this awareness go.

rather than becoming immersed in their existence. It is helpful to realize that you can connect to disconcerting thoughts
in the same way you can to relate to sounds. If you can begin
to liken your thoughts to external sounds, like a radio that's
been left on in the background, and decide not to turn up the
volume, then you can free yourself from the hold that your
thoughts may have over you.

Music
Listening to music is a great way to de-stress and to help you
to reconnect with your breath and body. For some people,
staying still and bringing attention to thoughts and sounds can
be tremendously challenging. Often, if we are feeling tense,
the thought of any sort of meditation can seem like a ridicu-
lous prospect. However, music can bring us a new, creative
and sometimes empowering energy. When we focus on the
beats, lyrics, bass or instrumental backdrop to any piece of
music, we can be wholly engaged in the present moment and
this can help us quieten our tirade of thoughts.

Everybody's association to music is different and how much
we listen, play or dance to it varies from person to person.
Much like our ability to change our tone, mannerisms and
speech depending on who we are talking to, we can adapt our
musical tastes to suit our mood or situation. Take a moment
to think about your relationship with music and how it affects
your frame of mind. Tapping into those moments when you

hear a song that prompts an emotional response is a useful way to acknowledge and accept your feelings in that very instant. Perhaps once the tune has finished the emotion softens or maybe it loiters? Recognizing how external factors influence our thoughts and feelings is a useful way to understand the variable nature of our minds.

There are many occasions when you can mindfully listen to music, whether you are in the kitchen, in a car or café, or at a party or gig. As music is often the underpinning sound of many social situations, if you find yourself feeling anxious or stressed, you could use the tune playing as an anchor to steady your breath and thoughts. Note the speed of the music, the different instruments that combine to make the sound, the changes in pitch and volume, and the meaning of the lyrics. Try to bring your attention to how your body responds: does your heart beat faster? If the music is loud, can you feel vibrations in your chest? Observe if a song is linked to a memory and whether you start reminiscing about the past. Does the music and volume exacerbate your anxiety or reduce it? Notice these thoughts, then let them go. Try to bring your awareness back to the music.

MINDFUL EXERCISE

MUSIC MEDITATION
THREE MINUTES

You can apply mindful listening to music in your own personal space. The advantage of this short mindful exercise is that you can do it every day in most settings.

• Choose any song or short piece of music that you enjoy and let yourself become absorbed in its vitality. A tune usually lasts only a few minutes so make sure you dedicate this time to the sole act of listening.

• It may be helpful to close your eyes and use headphones to keep out any external distractions. Whatever emotions, feelings or thoughts arise, be aware of these with an open and non-judgemental mind. Note what it is happening mentally and physically when you listen to a piece of music.

• Let these sensations rise and then evaporate so that you can be brought back into your musical zone, where there are only the sounds that are occurring in the here and now.

• When the music has finished, note how you feel by bringing your attention back to your breath, body and thoughts. Do you feel at peace? Frustrated? Relaxed? Is there a shift in your outlook and feelings after listening to the music?

It is valuable to reflect on how you feel pre- and post-meditation because this can give you the incentive to do it again or to change anything that didn't work for you. Maybe next time you will choose a more melodic piece of music or one with more meaningful lyrics.

CHAPTER FIVE

KNOW YOURSELF

*Despite the word 'mind' in mindfulness,
the aim of the practice isn't to engage with
thoughts. Instead, the intention is to focus on senses
and sensations that arise in and around us. We need
to be able to recognize the significant role our
emotions have on our bodies so that we can know
ourselves better. If we can learn to pay attention
to the physical feelings associated with our
emotions, this will help to relieve physical
and mental pain.*

CHANGING PERCEPTIONS

Your body is not something to be fragmented into certain parts to be liked and disliked. It is whole, we live in it, and it functions naturally in just the right way. Learning to accept and love ourselves starts with identifying the fact that our minds have a considerable effect on how our bodies work.

IN CHILDHOOD, WE ARE GENERALLY FREE in our bodies. For most of us, there was once a time when we could dance, run, jump, walk or skip with confidence. Our bodies were the best vehicles for our abundance of energy and we lived in them with innocence and unfaltering love. Our basic needs were usually met: when we were hungry we would eat, when tired we would sleep and when active we would move. What is more, the body was something that was whole and not broken into separate pieces to be flaunted or hidden or scrutinized.

It is only as we grow older, when we are taught the 'right' and expected way to talk, eat, sit and express ourselves, in relation to our gender, age, class, beliefs and culture, that we may begin to conform to societal pressures and norms. Once we start to view the body as something that can be moulded to suit our desires and expectations, we become detached from the natural purposes of our body and instead see it as an object that can be improved, reconstructed and reshaped.

Faced with this constant quest to fix what we find wrong with ourselves, we begin to lose our connection to the basic functions of our body: the breath, heartbeat, digestion, limbs, muscles and organs. Instead, we label what we like and dislike about our physique. With this loss of contact with the true nature of our bodies, we may not be aware when, how and why we hold tension, trauma, pain and suffering. If we can change our relationship with our bodies, we can ease the pressure to be perfect and rekindle a kinder, simpler connection to ourselves. We may also find that by acknowledging that our emotions are held in the body, we can release some of our tension and feel the body's capacity to move and pulsate with life.

With this loss of contact with the true nature of our bodies, we may not be aware when, how and why we hold tension, trauma, pain and suffering

By learning to be content in our bodies, we can relax and pay full attention to the variety of sensations that flow through us. If we become lost in critical thoughts about ourselves, our bodies will respond; if we are not aware of the relationship between mind and body, this can lead to further physical strain. It is through meditation that we can learn to accept our thoughts and hopefully our bodies, so that we can be more peaceful and composed, mentally and physically.

YOUR MIND & BODY

◆

As a student you often experience a lot of changes simultaneously: starting university or college, moving away from home and forming new relationships. Consequently, you may find yourselves out of your comfort zone on numerous occasions, which may play havoc with your confidence and self-esteem.

Mixing with new peers can lead to social anxiety, and you may find that you begin to form a new identity. Some are able to breeze through the fluctuations of life, but for many people, change is hard. However you respond emotionally to change, it can be guaranteed that your body is also reacting to the ups and downs of life events. The voice in our minds is like a puppeteer controlling how our bodies respond.

Recognizing the relationship between the mind and the body could help you to be better equipped to deal with life in all its many colours and to untangle a stuck mental state. Sometimes, when we are caught up in a mesh of negative and ruminating thoughts, it is extremely difficult to accept that these thoughts are not real. You have heard them so relentlessly repeated in your mind that they have become facts. Often, when we are trapped in this self-deprecating spiral, it will have a huge impact on our bodies. With such defeatist thinking, you may find that you have tension in your neck or grind your teeth. If you pay attention to the association between your thoughts and the physical sensations they arouse then perhaps you can begin to shift your emotional state.

When we gently ask ourselves how we feel physically rather than getting lost in our pessimistic worries, anxieties or fears, it may transpire that our hearts are racing, our palms are sweaty or our breathing is shallow. By focusing on the sensations in our bodies, rather than the thoughts in our minds, we can begin to free ourselves from torment because we now have a new focus.

If you can become aware of the physical feelings that occur naturally in the body and can pay attention to what you can see, hear, feel, taste and touch, you will be in sync with what is really happening in your body and mind. By transferring your attention away from your thoughts and noticing how your body responds in moments of crisis, you will not be drawn into an emotional swamp. Notice that physical sensations don't last – for example, your heart won't continually race at one hundred miles per minute and you won't be a dripping sweat ball forever. This will help you to accept that just as physical sensations change, fade and then eventually disappear, so will your distressed mental state.

Next time you experience a negative emotion, try bringing attention to how your body has responded. If you feel anxious, or simply remember a situation in which you felt anxious, your body reacts. Your chest may feel heavy or you may begin to feel nauseous. Once you are aware of what your body is doing, you can begin to calm yourself down. Take some deep breaths, get some fresh air or tune into the sounds and smells around you as a way to help ground yourself back in the present moment.

If you are able to calm your body, you are able to calm your mind. Even though your physical sensations may seem over-powering, try to stay with them, because ignoring them or trying to battle against them can often only exacerbate what you are feeling. If your thoughts are fighting their way to the forefront of your mind, note the thoughts, accept them and then visualize them passing by. Now, go back to how your body has responded. With an awareness of how you feel phys-ically, with time, these sensations will lessen, as will your attachment to your emotion.

EXERCISE

Regular exercise helps you to reconnect with your body, increases confidence and benefits your overall health. When it is done mind-fully a whole new, deeper dimension is added.

EXERCISE DOESN'T HAVE TO BE about losing weight or toning your body. It can be a gentle activity that lifts your spirit and bonds you with nature. During highly stressful times close to deadlines, exams, presentations or interviews, exercise can help to reduce panic or anxiety because it is a productive outlet for emotions. University is an ideal time to experiment with a new sport, and the team spirit of a group game can lead to long, dependable relationships. Applying a mindful approach to an activity can improve alertness and help you to tune in with the tactics and abilities of your teammates and opponents, which makes it more likely that you will win!

You can choose to exercise mindfully in any sport you enjoy. Here I suggest three that work well with mindful attention: walking, swimming and running.

Walking

Walking has been used within the practice of mindfulness for centuries and you can do it every day, for free. Even if you are caught up in your studies and feel too pressurized to step outside for a break, you could try mindfully pacing indoors at home. The aim of mindful walking is to be aware of how you move and breathe as you walk as well what you can see, smell and hear. You can walk fast if you like: you don't have to move at a snail's pace to be

Exercise doesn't have to be about losing weight or toning your body. It can be a gentle activity that lifts your spirits

alert and aware of your surroundings. If you can apply this attentiveness to the act of walking, then perhaps you can use it in everyday life too.

MINDFUL EXERCISE

WALKING MINDFULLY
5–15 MINUTES

You can easily bring mindfulness to the way you walk. This could be a brief mindful exercise or could last the duration of your journey from A to B. Each time you go for a walk you could try and extend the amount of time you spend in a mindful zone.

• Start by bringing attention to your feet moving along the floor or ground. Then notice your arms. Are they flapping along your side as you walk? Are they folded or rigid? Try to relax them.

• What is your posture like? Try relaxing your shoulders and lifting your head so that you can take in the world with an air of self-assurance.

• Once you have established your style and posture, bring your attention to your environment. What can you see? Whether you are walking on a bustling street or within the stillness of nature, notice how with each step, the scenery, sounds and smells will slightly change. Move and be at one with these transitions, not thinking about your endpoint but being receptive to what you can see, hear and smell in the here and now.

The advantages of this simple exercise are that it soon becomes second nature and you can do it every day in most settings.

Swimming

Swimming is the perfect form of exercise to apply mindfulness because this activity relies on how you use your breath. As you dip your head in and out of the water, focus on your inhalation and exhalation. Depending on how you swim, when you exhale you may blow bubbles under water. This unique sensation is even more enjoyable when you are fully aware of how your breath creates movement in the water. Bring attention to the way your body glides, stretches and splashes as you move across and through the water. Perhaps you want to take a moment to feel your body floating on the water's surface.

Even better is the revitalizing and energizing experience of swimming outdoors in a swimming pool, river, lake or the sea. As your face meets the fresh, crisp air after resurfacing for the first time, you will feel an array of sensations.

Running

It is normal for our minds to wander when performing any sort of exercise. Sometimes when we run, our minds run with us. But the aim of any mindful form of workout is to merge your physical and mental focus. This can begin with noting how you feel before you set out for your jog or sprint. By acknowledging your mental state prior to setting off you may find that you won't be so distracted by situations that affect how you feel.

MINDFUL EXERCISE

EXERCISING MINDFULLY

Use these basic steps to help achieve a physical and mental focus for your exercise session. Be kind to your body by taking care of it and not pushing it to its limit.

• Note how you feel before you start. If you are feeling anxious, down or worried, begin your routine by taking some deep breaths. This will help to reduce your emotional stress so you can focus on your activity with full attentiveness.

• Wherever you are exercising, be aware of your surroundings by taking in the smells, sights and sounds around you.

• Notice how your temperature and heartbeat change during the activity. Do your muscles ache or feel stretched? Are they enjoyable sensations? Do they trigger an emotional response?

• Be aware of your thoughts as you exercise. Are you able to return easily to your physical sensations?

• Be aware of your posture as you exercise since this affects how you move and feel.

• Keep focusing on the flow of your inhalation and exhalation to anchor you in the present moment. Be curious and non-judgemental about how it changes rhythm and intensity as you exercise.

• How do you feel once you have completed your activity? Are you calmer or more energized? Does your body hurt or feel more relaxed?

Because running is a high-impact activity, your breath, body, muscles, heart rate and speed will change considerably throughout your journey. Be aware of these changes and be conscious if you are pushing through any pain. How do you feel once these changes and sensations occur? Does it make you relieved? Angry? Free? Knowing how running helps your emotional well-being allows you to use this to your advantage and to accept how you feel rather than using exercise as a form of escapism. As with the walking exercise on page 104, you can use what you see, hear and feel to ground you in the present moment while you run.

PHYSICAL PAIN

Meditating cannot take away physical pain but it can help to change the psychological relationship with suffering and allow you to manage pain more effectively.

You may be suffering from chronic pain, a sports injury, headache, stomach ache or another form of discomfort. Often, enduring physical pain can lead to negative thinking because you become frustrated, annoyed, disappointed and let down by the debilitation of your body. You will probably have to take painkillers. Yet even if the pain is reduced, the ruminating, negative thinking associated with the pain can still exist.

If you can bring mindful attention to your physical feelings, you may learn to accept and cope with suffering. It may seem counterintuitive to focus on physical pain as a way to deal with it. But if you are able to turn towards the pain and not avoid or fight against it, you may find that the raw sensations in your body are not as powerful as you thought. Sometimes, it is the coupling of the thoughts and the pain that make our outlook and experience worse. If we can eliminate the negative thought patterns associated with pain, we may find that we can be more tolerant of unpleasant feelings. Instead of reprimanding ourselves for what we believe to be the failures of our bodies, we can enhance our self-compassion.

MINDFUL EXERCISE

MEDITATION FOR PAIN MANAGEMENT
FIVE MINUTES

This meditation helps you to turn towards painful sensations to challenge unhelpful thinking; it may make the pain more manageable.

• Whether you are lying down, sitting or standing, choose to be fully at one with this experience, even if just for a few seconds.

• Momentarily try to let go of any thoughts about the past or future. Try to focus on the present moment by bringing attention to your breath, and the sounds and smells around you.

• Briefly scan your body by focusing on each part and pause where you feel pain. Breathe into the unpleasant feelings and become aware if you have started to add a layer of thinking to your pain. Try instead to feel the pure sensations of the discomfort rather than analysing it. Notice if your mind is able to move away from the ache or whether you have become fixated on it.

• Be aware of the labels you have used in your head to describe what you are feeling. Perhaps you are thinking how excruciating the pain is or how it feels like torture or agony. The vocabulary we use to define our pain can affect our association with it. Instead, when you come across your pain, try calling it by a different name, such as a discomfort, wave or throb. Does changing the vocabulary affect how you feel about it?

• Move away from the focus on your pain and pay attention to the body working as a connected whole. Maintain this awareness for a few minutes by focusing on your body breathing as one.

CHAPTER SIX

COMPASSION

*Self-compassion and mindfulness are
intrinsically linked since meditating is itself
an inward act of care and kindness. Similarly,
both recognize that suffering is part of the human
condition and that to overcome hardships, we must
non-judgementally accept and acknowledge our
emotional state of mind. Compassion begins with
yourself. It is a wish to be free of suffering, to be kind
and to want the best for yourself. Once this feeling is
well rooted, it can be enhanced and extended out to
others. Compassion fosters emotional intelligence and
in turn deepens and improves all relationships. At its
best, self-compassion can have a rippling effect within
society; the aim is to cultivate happiness, love and
kindness to all of humankind.*

SELF-COMPASSION

Change can alter your sense of self and can positively or negatively affect how you view or even treat yourself. Being a student, it is likely that you are forging new directions in your life and new relationships. This is exhilarating, but with change comes uncertainty about who you are and what you will become. Self-compassion helps you to feel more secure in yourself.

FOR YEARS, EDUCATION AND RESULTS have weighed heavily on your day-to-day existence. With such value placed on success in exams, the teaching of how to be kind and compassionate towards yourself is usually forgotten. As a student facing new social and academic pressures and expectations, you will need to learn to cope with challenges, personal mistakes and failures.

When forming new friendship groups, you may find that acceptance is based on status or social, religious or cultural norms. If you do not fit the standard mould of the group, you may feel rejected. Since university life is a massive step up from college or school, you may begin to feel out of your depth academically. Your academic performance may begin to deteriorate as the workload increases and decent grades might feel unattainable. If you feel you are not doing well in comparison to students who seem more intelligent than you, your fears of failure are ignited. If you begin to believe the

Self-esteem and Self-compassion

It is easy to confuse self-esteem and self-compassion. When we have high self-esteem, this frequently comes from doing well and achieving our goals. As a student, it may feel that you are constantly trying to achieve your grades or goals in your career development, and as a result your self-esteem can be knocked in all directions. Your self-esteem can change from one moment to another. One minute you receive an excellent test result and feel elated; the next minute you argue with a friend, and your self-esteem plummets.

If self-esteem is measured by our own success and failures, it is understandable that at times we can feel second-rate and even more so when we begin to compare ourselves with others. In school, the first question I always hear whenever I hand back test results is the murmur in the classroom of 'What did you get?' It is as if we can only base our own worth against someone else's.

Self-compassion differs because it helps when things don't go plan or when we feel let down. What's more, it moves us away from our comparative frame of mind and instead focuses on the similarities we have with others. If we are able to stop comparing we may find that our own achievements are worthy in their own right.

LOVING-KINDNESS MEDITATION
THREE MINUTES

This meditation is helpful if you are feeling antagonized by others. It may be hard to send positive and caring energy to those you resent or have caused you pain. But in time it can improve self-acceptance and help you overcome resentment and anger.

• Find a quiet space in which to sit comfortably, close your eyes and take a few deep breaths.

• Think to yourself, 'I am just right, just as I am.'

• Say quietly, 'May I be happy. May I be safe. May I be healthy, peaceful and strong. May I give and receive gratitude.'

• Stay with these thoughts of loving kindness for a few moments.

• If your mind drifts, repeat the phrases.

• Change your thoughts to focus on someone you care about, someone who is suffering or someone you disagree with.

• Try cultivating feelings of love, kindness, appreciation and care towards your chosen person.

• Quietly say, 'May you be happy. May you be safe. May you be healthy, peaceful and strong. May you give and receive gratitude.'

• Gently open your eyes and feel assured that you can come to these loving and friendly feelings and thoughts at any point in your day.

voice in your head that says you are inadequate, you may find that you are creating your own downfall. When you feel as if you have let yourself down, negative thoughts can spiral.

To reach a point at which you are able to shift your inward perception, it's important to start by recognizing how you respond in moments of personal crisis. For example, if your heart is broken, are you left feeling anxious and depressed? Are you struck with fear if there is a big change in your life? Sometimes personal suffering can lead to a fixed mindset – for instance, 'things always go wrong for me' – and it can be hard to prevent discouraging thoughts. These thoughts can circulate like bad dust in a locked room and can go unnoticed because we become so used to them. It is essential that we recognize and acknowledge our unhelpful mindset so that eventually we can learn to accept, heal and move on.

Self-compassion can help deal with this emotional pain – in particular, meditation that focuses on generating inner love and kindness. This helps you to develop feelings of love and kindness towards yourself. During negative and self-critical moments, you can choose to adopt a kinder approach to yourself. You can do this by thinking about what you would advise someone you care about if you saw them suffering. Being self-compassionate means using this kind voice for yourself. One of the aims of meditating with love and kind-ness in mind (both for ourselves and others) is to cultivate a positive sense of well-being.

What's more, mindfulness and self-compassion teach us that we do not live in isolation but that our actions have a knock-on effect within society. Our moods, although we may feel that they are very much internal, are projected onto those around us and as a result can affect how others think and feel about themselves. If we are able to recognize our own suffering and instead adopt a kind, loving and compassionate approach towards ourselves, this can feed into all our relationships. It can have a transformative effect on all those around us, as well as enabling us to overcome personal setbacks. In time, the aim is to want the happiness you desire for yourself for all other human beings.

At the core of loving-kindness meditation is the aim to view everyone as equal and to see that despite obvious differences we are all just human beings.

UNDERSTANDING OURSELVES

Knowing that our moods and emotions determine our happiness is not helpful when we feel unhappy. When we fall short of our desired emotional state, we can end up judging ourselves. However, if we are unhappy, it is not our fault and we should not blame ourselves.

OUR BRAINS ARE COMPLEX and all our emotions, the positive and the negative, are part of our evolution. We have two parts of the brain: the old and new. The old part of the brain helped early humans to survive and is based on emotions, behaviour such as aggression, and making relationships. The new part is based on imagination, rumination, planning and thinking. Two million years ago, the brain evolved thinking in new ways, which formed the ability to imagine and fantasize. This created a sense of self and the ability to reason and think. These abilities can be used productively, and they make the world what is it today.

Nonetheless, these same abilities can also cause us internal conflict. We can ruminate about our sadness or create a sense of self that is unworthy and inferior. We create a self-identity and can be governed by the perception we have of ourselves. Perhaps we see ourselves as 'clever', 'unlucky' or 'a failure'. Once we have formed and believe in our created identity, it can become hard to move away from it, no matter how harsh or damaging it may be.

Although we have the skills to control unpleasant emotions (through mindfulness and tapping into our 'being mode' – see chapter two), the old part of our brains often forces us back to feeling threatened, anxious or angry. As a result, these instinctive emotions are at the forefront of our thinking, imagining and feeling. Imagine that next week you have your final exam at university. Undoubtedly, you feel anxious and as a result all you can think about is the exam and the many ways it could go wrong. The ambition to succeed floods your body with sensations and encourages you to act: you may study extremely hard and revise all night. The feeling of anxiety directs your trail of thoughts, reasoning and focus so much that you are utterly consumed with the dreaded exam. It may feel that you do not have control of your emotions, so you just go with them. You may think that you will feel better once the exam is over, but in the meantime you have bitten away at your nails and haven't slept properly for days. The more we think about our anxiety, the more anxious we become. It is a dangerous, vicious cycle that can feel impossible to break.

Self-compassion offers an alternative viewpoint. When we are mindful we can step away from our thoughts and choose not to be dictated by them. Taking this one step further, if we practise self-compassion we can learn to recognize that our inner critic only perpetuates our fears and instead we can choose purposefully to redirect and reframe our thoughts so that they are helpful to us.

If an experience during childhood made us feel anxious, later in life when we feel this same emotion again, we may find we react in a similar way. Instead of feeling the emotion in isolation, we automatically go into self-protection mode. We form our own protection strategies in order not to feel hurt or attacked. We may become more aggressive or choose to avoid the issue, close down or become submissive. If, for example, presenting to a group makes you anxious and you associate the feeling of anxiety with a hurtful memory, you may avoid doing presentations at all costs or burn yourself out by working too hard in an attempt to perfect your public-speaking skills. You can become locked into a negative way of thinking as your old anxieties overlap with your new ones.

However, if we only listen to the one-sided voice in our heads that feeds our anxiety, we receive a biased view of our situation or feelings. This voice can be strong-willed and persistent, which in turn can lead to a damaging opinion of ourselves. Learning to pay attention to our compassionate voice or self can be beneficial when we feel trapped or even controlled by our unpleasant emotions. Through practice, eventually we will start to think and behave in such a way that balances out or counteracts unhelpful thoughts and emotional patterns.

Applying the Skills of Self-compassion

Being self-compassionate means learning to direct our focus in a way that is helpful. For example, if you are feeling disappointed in yourself, can you shift your attention to something that is positive? You could focus instead on what you have achieved to date or praising yourself for your friendships.

Try to think more kindly about your relationships and circumstances. If you find yourself ruminating on your resentments, regrets or anger, can you redirect your thought processes? Try asking yourself, 'What is a better way to think about this issue?'

When you are overcome with stress, try to behave in a kind and compassionate way towards yourself. Try to recognize when you are stuck with your studies and ask for the support of others if you are not coping well.

Aim to reciprocate with help and support for your peers if they are having difficulties. Alleviating suffering is at the core of self-compassion.

Behaving in a compassionate way may mean trying new things and stepping out of your comfort zone – the aim is to move away from prejudice and judgement.

Self-criticism

In our bid to be successful, we are often our own worst enemies. Eager to do well, to excel and to contribute to society, we can put undue pressure on ourselves. If we don't achieve what we aim for or feel that we aren't as intelligent as our peers, we don't need a condemning teacher to wag their finger at us and tell we aren't good enough. Our own inner critic is already repeating the catchphrase at full volume. Just as we feel threatened, downtrodden and useless if others criticize us, we also feel this way when we criticize ourselves. We may be so used to our punitive voice that we do not realize that it is activating our stress systems and triggering feelings of anxiety, depression or anger. This self-critical voice may temporarily spur us on and give us some extra fight. However, if our negative voice is constantly present, we will feel constantly threatened, which in the long term can deter us from achieving our goals.

Often we are the most self-critical when we feel we have failed to achieve something or when we do not present ourselves in the way we would like – we might worry that we come across as timid or boring when we meet new people. At moments when we feel we have let ourselves down, we can be particularly harsh on ourselves. The first step in choosing to behave compassionately towards your-self is to know that your inner self-critic is a cause of higher stress levels and anxiety. If you can learn to question your unpleasant feelings or recognize how hard your situation is with a sense of compassion, you can achieve a sense of balance rather than feeling flooded by your negative emotions.

Aim to reciprocate with help and support for your peers if they are having difficulties

Your Kind Voice

Just as we can feel contentment, safety and warmth when we are reassured, emotionally held and comforted by those who love and care for us, we can also generate these feelings from within. We all have an inner voice that is kind and compas-sionate, even if we haven't tuned into it yet. To help us cope with inevitable setbacks and failures, we can learn to send

Reframing Your Inner Critic

This exercise helps you to recognize when you are being self-critical and to reframe your negative voice.

• When you feel you have done something wrong, what does the voice in your head sound like? What is the tone? Which words are used? Maybe you call yourself an idiot after saying something you feel embarrassed by or you tell yourself you are stupid after you have failed a test.

• Think about the differences between how you speak to yourself and how you speak to people close to you. Would you speak to friends or family members in this critical way?

• Make an effort to change your tone and words. It may be helpful to imagine what you would say to a friend if they were in the same situation.

• Next time you catch yourself being critical, what could you say that would change and soften your tone?

• Begin to see yourself as a friend or a young child that needs and wants nurture, kindness and love.

• If you can't find words of care or kindness, it is helpful to imagine or apply a physical touch of warmth, because this can release oxytocin, the 'love hormone', into your body. You could hug yourself or gently stroke your arm.

• Each time you catch yourself using condemning language, try to go back to your kind voice.

ourselves supportive and caring thoughts to help us through difficult times. You can practise taking an objective stance by thinking about what your grandmother, father or any other loving relative would say to you. Would they be as stern? What words of comfort might they offer? By thinking about a kinder approach, you can use your internal voice to rethink your situation.

COMPASSION TOWARDS OTHERS

Adopting a compassionate attitude requires responsibility and commitment and needs to be based on a sincere wish to free others of their suffering. If we want to practise compassion, we choose to reject violence and aggression and instead to have a mindset that is respectful and considerate towards everyone.

COMPASSION TOWARDS OTHERS is a feeling of sympathy towards somebody else's suffering and a strong desire to try to alleviate their pain. It is easier to feel compassion towards those you love or are close to. You may genuinely want the best for your friends and family and hope that they will be free from any form of suffering. Yet when love turns to hatred, our compassion can dissipate. If someone you care about betrays or hurts you, then your wish for their general well-being can quickly disappear as you are swamped by feelings of anger, resentment or bitterness.

When compassion is linked to emotional attachment towards someone, it is not truly genuine since it relies on your mental attitude and feelings towards that person. The Dalai Lama, the spiritual head of Tibetan Buddhism, argues that genuine compassion isn't a feeling towards those you know and care about, but a desire for all human beings to be happy and free from suffering: friend, stranger or even enemy. It is when you can see yourself reflected in others and imagine yourself in the same situation, no matter how alien it is to you, that you can nurture authentic compassion.

When you move away from home or start university, your world expands. You may meet people from cultures and religions that are unfamiliar to you. Perhaps you will be exposed to other people's hardships. If you are able to offer love and kindness to everyone you meet – old and new friends, and even individuals you don't like – then you are able to connect to others on a deep level. In turn, this gives you a fresh outlook on life.

Compassion & Empathy

Although compassion and empathy are similar, there is a stark difference between them. Empathy is understanding what another person might be feeling. When that other person is truly suffering, we understand what they are going through, but our care and help stop there. Compassion is going one step further and taking on that pain so that we feel it too and need to do something to help.

Sometimes we empathize, but in order to protect ourselves from suffering, we do not offer compassion because it is too much to handle. I have a friend whose mother is very ill. When she was telling me about the time she spent in hospital by her side I felt as if I understood her pain and could imagine how awful it was for her. However, I could not quite bring myself completely to embody her pain. I wanted to be a good friend, a good listener and to be there for her, and I believe on some level I achieved this. Yet if I had been compassionate, if I had been able to suffer with her, it may have reduced her own sorrow. Learning compassion is a skill just like being mindful, and when practised enough, it can change how our brains work so that we find being compassionate comes more easily to us.

CHAPTER SEVEN

STRESS-LESS

*During highly stressful times, tapping into
your own mindful resources will lift pressure and
give you the coping mechanisms to handle challenges.
If you meditate regularly or bring yourself to mindful
awareness for brief moments, you will find that you can
manage at times of heightened stress, such as taking
exams or making fundamental life decisions. This final
chapter consolidates what has been explored
throughout the book and suggests further
ways to apply mindfulness skills.*

MINDFULNESS EVERY DAY

❖

For even the most chilled-out students, life at university can be stressful. There is so much to deal with from homesickness, loneliness and relationship difficulties to juggling part-time work with studies and revising for exams. If you can achieve a mindful state of mind through short and achievable meditations and mindfulness exercises, you will find that your stress levels decrease.

EVERYONE HAS DAYS WHEN IT ALL FEELS too much. When I feel overwhelmed, I long to spend the day under my duvet watching brain-numbing TV programmes and munching junk food. However, this is rarely feasible. There are deadlines to meet, people who rely on me and an employer who pays me. Sometimes, what initially feels like the easy option ends up being the hard one. It is when we are most stressed that we begin to catastrophize: 'I will never get this done', or 'I'm going to fail at everything'. The trick is to know when your stresses have begun to dictate your actions – you are either overworking or procrastinating – and acknowledge that there is a way out. This offers you a productive route towards a healthy and balanced mind that can deal with the kaleidoscope of student life.

If you are able to shift your thoughts, the time and energy spent stressing over every potential awful outcome can be reassigned. Instead of thinking, 'There is too much to do', you can think how to make a dent in your heavy workload. With a mindful attitude, you will be focused in the present on what you are doing to meet your deadlines. Likewise, if you are finding it hard to socialize with new groups or feel out of your comfort zone, it is easy to dig yourself into a hole with pessimistic thoughts that people may not like you. This can result in missing out on opportunities to engage with other students, which can lead to feelings of loneliness and worthlessness. Recognizing that your thoughts are spiralling is a mindful act in itself. It's once we become aware that our thoughts are harmful that we can begin to do something about them.

Mindful Moments

When periods of independent study become too intense, even a short burst of mindfulness can help you focus. Try setting a timer on your phone or laptop every hour and take a break of one minute or even 30 seconds. Use this time to pay attention to your breath before returning to your work. You should find your stress levels drop and that you feel more relaxed.

When revising, you could use a mantra that keeps you alert and helps you to absorb the information needed to pass your tests. Using the rhythm of your breath to aid your memory is an effective way to stay mindful. For example if you need to remember a certain date, say 1979, you could breathe in for '19' and out for '79'. Not only will you be combining breath and memory but hopefully you will feel calm and measured when faced with retaining a multitude of facts.

A Moment of Mindfulness

When it feels like you're drowning in your work, it is easy to forget to be mindful. Focusing on everyday activities with awareness is an effective way to maintain a consistent mindful approach to life.

Washing hands

Most of us wash our hands several times a day in a habitual, distracted manner. If you use this frequent activity to find a moment of equilibrium and peace, you may find it has a positive impact on your day.

• Feel the temperature and smoothness of the water as it touches your skin.

• Be aware of your hands rubbing together as you swoosh the water in between your fingers.

• Take in the scent of the soap and how it feels as it foams on the surface of your skin, then rinses away.

Having a shower

You'll usually take a shower alone in a quiet setting, so it can be a great opportunity to tap into your typical patterns of thinking. Dedicate this time to being at peace at the beginning or end of the day.

- Feel the temperature and pressure of the water as it hits your body. If it helps, close your eyes and focus only on this sensation for a few seconds.
- Notice the direction, speed and movement of your thoughts. Is your mind active? Are you feeling sluggish? Be aware of the nature of your mind and then bring your attention back to the sensations of the water on your body.
- When drying yourself, you could do a very quick body scan (see page 71) by paying attention to each part of your body as you pat it dry.

Brushing your teeth

You may use brushing your teeth as a time to multitask. Instead, try to bring awareness to all the sensations of this activity.

- Notice the flavour and texture of the toothpaste as you brush.
- Stay focused on how your arm and hand move the brush across and up and down your teeth.
- Be aware of how your mouth feels once you have finished.

Other ways to apply mindfulness daily could be to mindfully insert passwords; scroll through pictures; switch lights on or off; or make a cup of tea.

Writing as a Release

If you feel you lack self-belief or become frustrated if you don't achieve your best, try keeping a journal.

• When you are in a self-critical mood, try to write down some of your thoughts. Then write down what the alternative thought or viewpoint could be.

• If you are finding it hard to adopt a softer attitude towards yourself, imagine that you are writing to a friend. You wouldn't allow your friend to be spoken to with animosity, so there is no reason why you should treat yourself as your own worst enemy. Write yourself a kind letter that highlights your achievements, your goals and the measures you are willing to take to get there.

• Jot down your trigger stress moments. For example, your trigger moments could be public speaking, exams, interviews or presentations. Write down what you feel physically in these moments. Also write down what thoughts typically come to your head and how you react to them. Being aware of how we respond mentally and physically to unfavourable situations is the first step to accepting that we find certain things difficult. It is at this point of acceptance that we can apply a self-compassionate stance or even be willing to let these emotions go.

OVERCOMING NERVES FOR PUBLIC SPEAKING

At points during your student career, you are likely to be asked to give a presentation or have an interview. When we are asked to stand up and speak in front of others, most of us feel vulnerable, exposed and nervous. Mindfulness does not push aside our worries but enables us to cope with our fears and to face them head on.

ONE WAY OF CONFRONTING OUR FEARS is to really get to know them. Begin by asking yourself what you are most scared of. Are you scared that you will sound stupid? Or that something will go wrong and people will laugh at you? Think to yourself: are my fears valid? Remind yourself that you have the ability to present yourself well otherwise you would not have been invited to do so. Try to put your fears into perspective and tap into your 'kind voice'. Think about what advice you would give to someone you care about.

Being well prepared will reduce your fears and nerves. You could prepare by practising in front of the mirror or presenting to a friend. It's helpful to think about what you may be asked so that you can respond confidently to questions. Even if you have prepared all you can, you may still feel nervous. This is a completely normal response. The important thing is not to let your nerves get the better of you. Remember: if you can tune into nervous feelings, you may be able to tune them out as well.

MEDITATION FOR PUBLIC SPEAKING
FIVE MINUTES

Deep breathing can settle nerves and help you to rebalance a frazzled mind. On the day of your presentation or interview, try to put yourself in a relaxed and calm state by practising this short meditation.

• Close your eyes and focus on your breath. Take three deep and deliberate inhales and exhales through your mouth.

• As you fully exhale through your mouth, imagine you are breathing out any tension.

• Now breathe in through your nose to the count of 5 and out through your nose to the count of 5. This rhythmic breathing will help steady your nerves. Do this for three minutes.

• Once you feel connected to your breath, visualize the presentation from the beginning to the end.

• Imagine that you enter the room with confidence and stand in front of your peers or future employers with a straight posture, speaking with a clear, assertive voice.

• Picture your audience being interested in what you have to say.

• Imagine the presentation/interview and your delivery as a success.

• Take a moment to note how you feel now after this visualization. What sensations can you feel in your body?

• Is there a critical voice creeping its way to the surface?

• Notice the thought, consider it to be an external voice (not your own) and give it a name, 'Oh that's Frederick again'. Notice how this made you feel, then try a different voice or thought: 'I am able to present and I won't come across as stupid. What I have to say is important and it will be engaging.'

• Try again to visualize yourself presenting well both in content and delivery.

• For a few moments, go back to the rhythm of your breath.

MANAGING EXAM STRESS

◆

Exams and stress go hand in hand. Stress can be that helpful big sister pushing you on. However, it is essential to recognize when your stress or anxiety levels are preventing you from working productively.

D URING YOUR FIRST EXAM SEASON, you may feel alone and out of your depth. Perhaps it seems that your peers are able effortlessly to combine studying, socializing and taking part in sports while you are struggling to revise just one module. You may begin to feel that your whole life rests on your exams, because without a good degree you are afraid you will not get a decent job. You may even worry that you will lose your friends' respect if you don't achieve good grades. Alternatively, you may feel that exams are a horrible burden that is stopping you from enjoying yourself. Whether you are stressed because you're working too hard or not working enough, it is normal for these feelings to knock your confidence and exhaust your mind.

It is easy to think that the more time you spend working, the better your results will be. Yet if you are trying to study with a head that is feeling crammed, suffocated and dazed, it doesn't really matter how many hours you put in. You are better off making sure you have a clear and focused mind so that what you revise is retained and you are able to organize and prioritize your workload.

Importantly, you need to recognize the difference between healthy and unhealthy stress levels. Signs that stress is taking over could be indicated in changes to sleeping or eating habits. Maybe you are not exercising or socializing as much as you used to. You could find yourself being irritable or irrational. One of the aims of mindfulness is to acknowledge and accept our emotions without judgement, and once we truly know how we are feeling, then we can act.

Mindfulness will help you unravel your worries, stresses and fears, which helps you to revise more effectively

Some ways to reduce stress could be to make studying a more enjoyable experience. Create a better working environment by decluttering your desk or study alongside hardworking friends. Regular breaks are important: for a brief pause, take your eyes from your book or laptop and gaze into the distance while focusing for a few minutes on your breath. Going for short mindful walks is also helpful. See if you can make space for a proper break, say a trip to the cinema, a gig or meal. When you return to your work, you will feel revitalized.

Avoid Comparing Yourself with Others

When we are mindful or practising self-compassion, we try to move away from a comparing frame of mind. This is essential when it comes to revising. When you are trying to cram a year's worth of lecture notes, your brain is already working at full capacity, and it doesn't need jibes such as, 'look at how well Sarah already understands the concepts', or 'Max always gets top marks, it's so easy for him'. If you compare yourself to those who you feel are more able, you may feel less motivated to work hard. Although it sometimes feels like it, remember that exams are not a competition, and you will succeed in your right. Try to acknowledge that comparing yourself makes you feel deflated and then mindfully adopt a self-compassionate approach. Exams are hard for everyone and even if some students seem unfazed by the deluge of assessments, we all have inner doubt. Mindfulness will help you unravel your worries, stresses and fears, which in turn helps you to revise more effectively.

Mindfulness in Exams

Even if you revise well, you may feel incapacitated when it comes to sitting the exam. Practising mindfulness regularly should give you the skills to overcome your nerves and anxieties. When you walk into the exam hall, try to forget about everyone else and use your breathing to go inwards to your calm and centred place. Begin by noticing the natural flow and rhythm of your breath. If your breath is feeling restricted, try breathing in for a count of five and exhaling through your mouth to count of five. Your exhalation should connect to your parasympathetic nervous system, which will help to reduce your nervousness. You can go back to this deep and deliberate breathing at any moment in the exam, and if your mind is racing, now is the perfect time to find your kind and compassionate voice.

THE UNKNOWN

Starting university or college is an enormous emotional leap and finishing can feel like an even bigger one. You are expected to come out the other end with a qualification that will lead to a job and yet you may not even have a clue what you want to do. Learning to be comfortable with the uncertainty of your future starts with being comfortable knowing that life is unpredictable.

WHEN YOU ARE MINDFUL you can learn to accept without judgement that life as a student is demanding and that it's OK and normal to feel fearful of change and uncertainty. So much at this stage of your life is unknown. What job will you have? Where will you live? Who will your partner be? What will you do after your studies? Some people go through their whole lives asking these questions or living in the unknown.

Although the unknown can be unnerving, it is this same inevitability of change and unpredictability that makes life exhilarating. Delving into the mysterious abyss of your future with a mindful attitude can inspire you to wade through unfamiliar territory with an open and flexible mind which in turn can help you confound the slings and arrows that life throws at all of us.

On the one hand, mindfulness teaches you that we all experience scary thoughts and situations and that all our emotions and fears are valid. We would not be humans if we didn't connect with unpleasant feelings. On the other hand, mindfulness teaches us that these scary thoughts are manageable and that we can move on from them with non-judgement and kindness. It is once you have the skills of mindfulness that your journey as a student and beyond becomes a thrilling adventure that can embrace both lows and highs with the same balance of calm awareness and acceptance.

FURTHER READING

◆

The Art of Happiness: A Handbook for Living The Dalai Lama and Howard C. Cutler (Coronet Books, 1999)

'The Brain's Default Network: Anatomy, Function, and Relevance to Disease' R. L. Buckner, J. R. Andrews-Hanna and D. L. Schacter (2008) *Annals of the New York Academy of Sciences* 1124 (1): 1–38

'Dispositional Mindfulness Co-Varies with Smaller Amygdala and Caudate Volumes in Community Adults' Adrienne A. Taren, J. David Creswell and Peter J. Gianaros (2013) PLOS ONE 8(5): e64574 https://doi.org/10.1371/journal.pone.0064574

The McDonaldization of Society: An Investigation into the Changing Nature of Contemporary Social Life George Ritzer (Pine Forge Press, 1993)

Mindfulness-Based Cognitive Therapy for Depression: A New Approach to Preventing Relapse Z. V. Segal, J. M. G. Williams and J. D. Teasdale (Guilford Press, 2002)

Training Our Minds In, With and For Compassion. An Introduction to Concepts and Compassion-focused Exercises Phil Gilbert (2010) wtm.thebreathproject.org

INDEX

ACKNOWLEDGEMENTS

◆

I am grateful to my son Sky who teaches
me every day what it really means to be mindful.
I would like to thank my husband, John, whose endless
encouragement gave me the confidence to write my first
book. I am indebted to my father, Alan, who was my second
pair of eyes when mine were too tired to spot mistakes and
who has always believed in me. Heartfelt thanks too to my
mother, Vivienne, whose effortless calmness and patience
is an inspiration, and to my mother- and father-in-law,
Brian and Marie, who by looking after
Sky gave me the time to write.

My incredible four sisters, Laura, Jessica,
Georgia and Lydia, are my constant support,
strength and role models.

I am also grateful to the team at Leaping Hare Press
for their help and for giving me the opportunity to write
on a subject that I am passionate about: Stephanie Evans,
Susan Kelly, Tom Kitch and Cath Senker.